Gerlinde Frey-Vor

Coronation Street: Infinite Drama and British Reality
An Analysis of Soap Opera as Narritive
and Dramatic Continuum

D1723552

Gerd Stratmann (Hg.)

HORIZONTE
Studien zu Texten und Ideen der europäischen Moderne

Band 5

Gerlinde Frey-Vor

CORONATION STREET: INFINITE DRAMA AND BRITISH REALITY

An Analysis of Soap Opera as Narrative and Dramatic Continuum

ꟲꟳꟴꞇ Wissenschaftlicher Verlag Trier

Die Deutsche Bibliothek - CIP Einheitsaufnahme

Frey-Vor, Gerlinde:
Coronation Street: Infinite Drama and British Reality
An Analysis of Soap Opera as Narritive and
Dramatic Continuum / Gerlinde Frey-Vor.-
Trier: WVT Wissenschaftlicher Verlag Trier, 1991
(Horizonte ; Bd. 5)
ISBN 3-922 031-59-5
NE: Frey-Vor, Gerlinde:; GT

Transkript Satz und Gestaltung:
Monika Dieckmann
Manuela Hildebrand
Sonja Vogel

Umschlaggestaltung: Marco Nottar

© WVT Wissenschaftlicher Verlag Trier
ISBN 3-922 031-59-5

Trier, 1991
WVT Wissenschaftlicher Verlag Trier, Postfach 4005
5500 Trier

No book can be written by solitary effort of the author. That is why I would like to thank everybody who inspired and assisted me during the work which led to this book. But my special acknowledgement goes to Charles Barr (University of East Anglia) for his formating advice.

Furthermore, I would like to acknowledge the inspiration and help received from the Centre for the Study of Communication and Culture and the British Film Institute.

I am also indebted to Granada Television and the Westdeutscher Rundfunk for their provision of material.

Thank you very much as well to Frieder Schuster for the skilfull preparation of the manuscript.

Finally, I would like to thank Professor Stratmann as the series editor for his interest in the topic and Dr. Otto (WVT) for his patience and professional advice.

Not surprisingly the book is dedicated to my husband Rainer Vor who supported me and showed good humour throughout the different stages of writing.

G. F.-V.

CONTENTS

0. INTRODUCTION

A little more than thirty years ago Tony Warren submitted the idea of a twice weekly continuous serial which eventually became *Coronation Street*, to the ITV (Independent Television) production company Granada. Warren who wrote the first twelve - and also occasional later episodes, used the following, now almost legendary phrase in the memo to sum up the serial:

> "A fascinating freemasonry, a volume of unwritten rules. These are the driving forces behind a working-class street in the north of England. *Coronation Street* sets out to explore these values and in doing so, to entertain."[1]

Almost since the time of its inception the serial has consistently attracted large audiences and has continually appeared among the top ten programmes in Britain, this implied on average more than 16 million viewers and frequently well over 20 million. After some draw-backs, particularly in the years from 1986 to 1988, *Coronation Street* presently continues to be one of the most popular programmes on British television.

The humorous admiration of some people in Britain for and the more serious devotion of others to the thirty-year-old piece of infinite drama, was on the occasion of its anniversary on 9 December 1990 also shared by celebrities inclusive of the Queen who sent a good luck message to the cast, while the Labour Party's deputy leader Roy Hattersley delivered a 'Coronation Street Birthday Lecture' at the Edinburgh Television Festival. At the end of that speech Hattersley coined the phrase "Coronation Street is a pretension free zone"[2], this means in reference to the viewers, people from all classes and professions admit they enjoy it.

As the authors of the 1981 British Film Institute *Television Monograph: Coronation Street*[3] expounded, the serial came out of a particular historical moment at the end of the 1950s and early sixties, which in Britain was marked by a dominant trend to Social Realism in literature, theatre and film.
A number of the images and literary and dramatic conventions which prevailed in the sixties have become absorbed into the basic narrative structure of *Coronation Street*, which is that of the continuous serial, or soap opera. That structure mediates the representation of more topical elements of British life in the programme and determines the mechanisms by which viewers make sense of the serial today.

The fictional *Coronation Street* is situated in the fictional Weatherfield an

---

[1] *Granada Television Information Sheet*, p. 1.

[2] "Roy pays homage to the Rovers Return". *The Independent* 27-8-90, p. 15.

[3] Richard Dyer et al., *Television Monograph: Coronation Street*, ((BFI) London, 1981).

alleged district of Greater Manchester. But everybody in Britain who is vaguely familiar with the serial knows that it was the now demolished Archie Street in Salford on which the writers and producers drew as model for the *Street*. Salford was not only the place where middle-class writer Tony Warren's legendary maternal grandmother[4] lived but also a town that had long before the serial, entered the Social History of the 19th century as "the very epitome of industrial ghettos, the 'classic slum' itself"[5], to which Frederick Engels refers in his *The Conditions of The Working Class in England in 1844*.

But *Coronation Street* in 1960 reverberated the essence of a later, though less painful era of working-class life, namely that of the first half of the 20th century. Authors like Richard Hoggart who with his 1957 book *The Uses of Literacy* contributed to the so-called Affluence Debate, described a working-class life style as it had developed particularly in the years of the depression during the 1930s. *Coronation Street* which is undeniably influenced by Hoggart's slightly nostalgic autobiographicalaccount in *The Uses of Literacy*, conserved some of those expressions for at least another decade.
The *Coronation Street* of 1990 is marked by the dilution of those expressions through some more compory images of affluence and aspiration brought about under the Thatcher reign. However, the serial is able to combat such dilutions by a set of self-regulatory mechanisms supported by its customary humour.

Coronation Street's place in British media history is undisputed and documented, for instance in a permanent exihibition in the London Museum of the Moving Image[6].
Yet, even though *Coronation Street* may be an appropriate object for a museum, it is not to be abandonned there.
A participient in a recent group discussion on soap operas suggested: "Coronation Street became a cult because it was so lower class and everybody watched it because of that (...) in the sixties it was something new and it then grew." Another participient added "It is something constant and people need constancy in there lives these days, as everything is changing all the time".[7]

Yet, despite the constancy of its appearance, *Coronation Street* has changed its texture over the years, though not necessarily in consistence with developments in real life.

The recent fundamental changes in the media systems of Britain and other

---

[4] cf. Tony Warren, *I Was Ena Sharples' Father*, (London, 1969).

[5] cf. Robert Roberts, *The Classic Slum: Salford Life in The First Quarter of The Century*. ((Penguin) Harmondsworth, 4. ed. 1980), p. 14.

[6] The Museum of the Moving Image is an extensive, modern museum of film and televsion which opened in London in 1988.

[7] The discussion group on soap operas with five Anglo/German couples was held by the author in April 1990.

European countries have also rendered the soap opera market more competitive and led to a diversification of the genre.

Not surprisingly, *Coronation Street* has become a model for other Social Realist Soap Operas in Britain and elsewhere, in addition to being exported to some 16 countries. However, due to its continuous nature, the serial in turn is also affected by the competitive interaction with other more recent long-running serials on British TV, in particular the BBC serial *EastEnders* but also imported soap operas from America and Australia.

This book is written from the perspective of a German whose long-term research interest in the soap opera form was fueled a number of years ago on becoming acquainted with *Coronation Street* and the remarkable loyalty which different groups of viewers devoted to the serial. That interest was further increased when the first German soap opera *Lindenstraße*, a 1985 version of *Coronation Street* adapted to a different culture, arrived.

The study is based on a M.A. thesis originally completed in 1986, which has been revised to take account of more recent developments in *Coronation Street* and its production context, the soap opera genre as a whole and the research on it. It sets out to describe *Coronation Street* as a component of what will be tentatively termed 'the international soap opera genre' and investigates the interaction of its long-established narrative structures with contemporary British life and the stimuli from a competitive media industry. Through the transcription and close-analysis of two pivotal episodes of the serial in the 1980s featuring the Ken/Deidre/Mike marriage crisis, and through giving some insight into the production context, the book documents and investigates key mechanisms operating in a continuous long-term narrative and discusses them as factors in the reception process, also in regard to their political dimensions. In addition, the book offers a comprehensive overview of the main strands of research on soap operas internationally, to which it still hopes to make a valid contribution.

1. THE MAJOR LINES OF RESEARCH ON SOAP OPERAS INTERNATIONALLY AND THE PURPOSE AND APPROACH OF THIS STUDY

1.1. The Major Lines of Research on Soap Operas[1]

Research on the soap opera has existed almost as long as there has existed research on the electronic media. Some important strands in media research in general and research on the soap opera in particular, were pioneered in the United States by researchers at the Paul Lazarsfeld Bureau of Applied Social Research at Columbia University. There Herta Herzog, Frank Stanton, Rudolf Arnheim and others conducted in the late 1930s and early 1940s the pivotal research on the American radio soap operas and their audiences.[2]

Another early study on viewers of soap operas was undertaken by two Chicago University anthropologists, W. Lloyd Warner and William E. Henry.[3]

Nevertheless, it was the research of the Lazarsfeld group, in part inspired and financed by the commercial radio networks CBS and NBC, which for over thirty years remained the definitive study of the soap opera audience.

For, in the following decades research on soap operas remained relatively scarce. In 1982, this lead Bradley S. Greenberg and colleagues to suggest that the empirical social sciences had neglected research on the soap opera. But not only had empirical social scientists neglected the soap opera genre, little research did exist in other disciplines either.

Since Greenberg's et al. suggestion of a research deficit, however, a continual string of studies on the neglected and often derided soap opera genre has emerged.

Initially, it were mainly content studies informed by the paradigms and methods of the empirical Social Sciences in the United States. One of their dominant procedures has been to investigate the representation of certain varaibles in soap opera in comparison with real life.

This approach was taken a step further by the contributors to the book with *Life on Daytime Television*[4] edited by Mary Cassata and Thomas Skill. Like some earlier studies by Bradley S. Greenberg and Nathan Katzman its primary method

---

[1] For a more comprehensive survey of research on soap operas and telenovelas cf. Gerlinde Frey-Vor, *Communication Research Trends* Vol. 10, 1+2 (1990).

[2] Paul F. Lazarsfeld and Frank N. Stanton, *Radio Research 1942-1943*, (New York, 1944).

[3] W. Lloyd Warner and William E. Henry, "The Radio Day-Time Serial: A Symbolic Analysis". *Genetic Psychology Monographs*, Vol. 37, pp. 3-71.

[4] Mary Cassata and Thomas Skill (eds.), *Life on Daytime Television: Tuning-In American Serial Drama*, (Norwood, NJ, 1983).

is content analysis though it also contains some work on soap opera audiences and an interview with Robert Short, Manager of Daytime Programmes for *Procter and Gamble Productions*.

The first chapter of the book summarizes a study on soap opera characters according to their demographics, lifestyles and interpersonal conflict-management skills. The research is conducted with the perspective that soap opera characters are potential role models for viewers.

One of the findings of the study is that women are slightly under-represented (49 %) in the daytime soap opera in relation to their actual share in the population (52 %). But in comparison with prime-time television where the female : male ration is 1 : 3, the day-time serials' representation of the two sexes seems to be much more balanced.

The representation of black characters in the soap operas (4.8 %), however, was considerably lower than their representation on prime-time television (9 %)and thus deviate significantly from their share in the total population (11 %).

Another conclusion is that women in soap operas are more likely to have a professional position (though in most cases lower profile jobs) than in prime-time programmes. Despite that, homemaking is found to be presented as an exclusively female activity.[5]

With regard to the marital status of soap opera characters the authors come to the conclusion: "The most surprising aspect of this category is that nearly 70 % of the characters in our study were either in a single or divorced state." The reason why this result was surprising for the authors, was their assumption that soap operas were determined by plots about romantic love which culminate in matrimony.[6]

The lifestyle of soap opera characters is defined according to 13 different life-style categories. However, 79 % of all characters analysed fall under five main lyfe-style categories: The *Chic Suburbanite* (21 %), the *Subtle Single* (20 %), the *Traditional Family Person* (19 %), the *Successful Professional* (10 %) and the *Elegant Socialite* (9 %).

The authors investigate different conflict-management skills in each life-style group and come to the conclusion "that only characters with a predominant focus on home and family-centered interests can deal with a disagreement in a positive interpersonal fashion"[7]. Rich, culturally oriented serial personalities whose prime interests are directed to goals outside of the family "are superficial, dogmatic, and primarily self-serving"[8].

Similar content analyses on the portrayal of other variables such as "Old Age", "Illness, Accidents, Violence and Death", "Sexual Behavior" and "Structures of Power in Two-Person Interactions" (this is the typical soap opera situation), are

---

[5] ibid., p. 11.

[6] ibid., p. 12.

[7] ibid., p. 13.

[8] ibid. p. 14.

also contained in the book.

While systematic content analysis provides important insights into thematic preoccupations and - developments within the soap opera genre and the representation of particular social groups by that prolific form of television, it often does not pay much attention to its specific characteristics as a fictional 'text'. That is why researchers who are informed by literary criticism and cultural studies have recently stressed the importance to study soap opera as an aestetic construct with a specific internal organisation and narrative conventions. The main theoretical approach which is chosen by those scholars is structuralism as, for instance, proposed by the French anthropologist Lévi-Strauss and and the semiotic theory of texts as developed by Roland Barthes, Umberto Eco and others.

To various degrees these theories are also informed by the narrative studies of Vladimir Propp and combined with Marxist approaches, in particular those of Antonio Gramsci, Louis Althuiser and Raymond Williams. An early application of such a combined approach to the study of soap opera is displayed in the collection of essays on *Coronation Street* by Richard Dyer and others[9].

But the most comprehensive book so far on the soap opera genre which is informed by a structuralist/semiotic approach in combination with the reader-response theory proposed by Wolfgang Iser and others, is Robert Allen's 1985 book *Speaking of Soap Opera.*
Allen focusses on the US-American daytime soap opera as a textual system with a specific history and historical variations brought about by social and commercial influences.
He strongly refutes a simple and immediate relationship between soap opera and reality, a relationship reflected, from his point of view, in the research based on the US tradition of empirical social science.
Allen maintains that "(...) grasping what soap opera has come to mean requires that we examine the discursive contexts within which it has been used."[10] He illustrates the different light his approach can throw on some of the results from quantitative content analysis. According to him, the disproportionally high number of characters with middle-class, professional identities in the soap opera (compared to their share in the US-American population), has to be related to the generic rules of the form because soap opera is determined by talk and preoccupied with personal interaction. Middle-class milieus and work environments cater more for these generic prerequirements than, for instance, a working-class setting[11].
Likewise, Allen suggests that the meaning of accidents, diseases, sexual behaviour, death and childbirth etc. depends on their function within the narrative. However, structural linguistics does not only conceive the sign as constituent of a syntag-

---

[9] Richard Dyer et al., *Television Monograph: Coronation Street*, (London, 1981).

[10] Robert Allen, *Speaking of Soap Opera*, (Chapel Hill, NC, 1985), p. 9.

[11] ibid., p. 74.

matic (combinatory) structure but also as part of a paradigmatic (associative) structure. The paradigmatic structure refers to the web of associative meanings that link characters, settings, plots and stories together. The viewer's knowledge of the rules of the genre as a whole imparts additional meanings to the narrative elements of individual episodes. The viewer is able to interpret present happenings on screen by reference to his or her store of accumulated knowledge about the previous interactions of the characters and past events. This is especially the case if a soap opera has been running for a long time.
Allen talks in this context of the "narrative excess" of soap opera.

It is interesting to note that Allen explains the under-representation of black characters and characters from other minority groups which has been elicted by content analysis, by referring to the so-called 'paradigmatic dilemma' which such characters apparently create. While non-white characters, according to Allen, can be employed without major difficulties in an immediate plot line, their full incorporation into the long-term soap opera structure which is mainly built around kinship -, romantic - and social relationships, seems to be problematic. Allen comments: "Unless a particular soap opera were to embrace interracial romance, marriage, and parentage as a community norm, the admission of a non-white character into full membership in the soap community would be impossible, since two of the three relational modes would be all but closed to him or her."[12]
This 'paradigmatic dilemma', however, is affected by external forces. "Especially, the producers' desire not to 'upset' large numbers of their target audience (white women) by extending the narrative boundaries of the soap opera world too far."[13]
This conclusion implies that despite his concept of soap opera as primarily a textual construct, Allen has the entire system in mind from which soap opera evolves. The system which brings about the 'soap opera text' is determined by its own historical evolution which is influenced by the respective production systems, commercial requirements and audiences.
Following Wolfgang Iser's reader-response theory, Allen uses the concept of the 'implicit reader', thus drawing attention to the fact that a soap opera 'text' is always put together with a particular audience in mind.
Allen proposes that changing soap opera audiences and their changing attitudes had a share in transforming the genre, for example in affecting the ways young people or women were presented.

He also stresses that the above-cited "narrative excess" of soap opera increases its plurisignificative possibilities and undermines a consistent ideological message. Allen, though being aware of the ideological implications of, for instance, the restricted social reality of the US serials (e.g. the preoccupation with middle-class life styles and the omission of references to socio-economic conditions), warns that "we must not confuse presumed ideological intent with either

---

[12] ibid., p. 75.

[13] ibid.

reader response or ideological effect"[14].

From about the middle of the 1980s the study of audiences emerged as a strong trend in the study of soap opera.

While already Herta Herzog's pioneering study on the radio daytime- serial listeners in 1942 had applied a uses and gratifications approach, quite a number of the more recent studies have further tested and developed that approach in the study of continuous serials.[15] Sometimes this approach is combined with the theory on cultivation effect.[16]

Partially in extension of the structuralist/semiotic concept of soap opera as a text with a presumed role in the production of cultural and social patterns, but partially also due to the influence of a family sociological approach to the uses and functions of the media in everyday life, there likewise emerged a range of more qualitatively oriented studies on the reception of soap opera.[17] These studies share with the uses and gratifications approach the concept of the active viewer. But unlike studies based on the latter approach, they do not aim at isolated social or psychological needs which soap opera watching may gratify. Instead, they endeavour to investigate the reception of soap operas within the social, historical, cultural and ideological patterns of viewers' lives.

Some results from the ethnographic research on soap opera viewing conducted by a German and American research team in West Origon may exemplify this kind of audience research.

Thus, Eva-Maria Warth, a member of the research team, looked at the West Oregon interview material to find evidence of the relation between daytime soap operas and house-work. She suggests that in the temporal organisation of industrialized society, which also embraces the domestic sphere, daytime serials (like television and radio in general) help to structure the house-wife's working day. A number of women conceded in the interviews that they arranged their house-work around their favourite soap opera. Warth, like other ethnographic researchers, stresses that there does not exist a clear spatial demarcation between work and leisure for the housewife. Watching soap operas can therefore mark an interval of leisure for the housewife. But the mode of watching differs considerably according to the style of work of different housewives. Only those who work highly organized (similar to the work routine in the public sphere) can allow themselves the luxury of sitting down and watching their favourite soap opera with undivided attention. Whereas housewives who do their work in a less structured

---

[14] ibid., p. 94.

[15] cf. for instance Alan M. Rubin, "Uses of Daytime Television Soap Operas by College Students". *Journal of Broadcasting and Electronic Media*, 29,3 (Summer 1985).

[16] cf. for instance Carveth Rodney and Alison Alexander, "Soap Opera Viewing Motivations and The Cultivation Process". *Journal of Broadcasting and Electronic Media*, 29,3 (Summer 1985).

[17] cf. for instance some contributions to: Ellen Seiter et al. (eds.), *Remote Control: Television Audiences and Cultural Power*, (London, New York, 1990) and to James Lull (ed.), *World Families Watch Television*, (London, New Delhi, Newbury Park, CA, 1988.

way (similar to the pre-industrial way of working) often do not manage to preserve a small space of leisure to watch a soap opera with full attention.
"The soap opera text becomes reduced to what can be heard while working in different parts of the house."[18]

Dorothy Hobson observed and interviewed six office women in Birmingham to investigate the role of talk about soap operas at work, which especially in Britain is a significant feature of the soap opera reception. Hobson concludes that talking about soap opera at work fulfills several functions: firstly, it provides moments of leisure in work; secondly, it helps to keep viewers informed on soap opera events and strengthens their critical ability; thirdly, it is part of the group process at the place of work.[19]

The fact that soap operas were originally designed as advertising vehicles to attract housewives has dubbed them a female genre.
This image is only barely modified by the fact that men, in particular young men (eg. college students), also watch soap operas if they are at home during the time of broadcast. Soap Operas have often been referred to with disdain not only because they are a form of popular mass fiction but also, as some researchers suggest, because they are associated with the world of women. This is more true of the American daytime serials than of prime-time - or early prime-time serials. Derry suggests that the mere words 'soap opera' (meaning daytime serial in the United States) binds those programmes to a sphere which is held socially unimportant, namely that of women's work. Furthermore, they are held to reflect a "sentimental, escapist and/or hysterical sensibility".[20]

Yet, the specific appeal which the soap opera seems to have for women has aroused the interest of feminist researchers.
An early example is Tania Modleski's textual analysis of American soap operas, which is informed by a psychoanalytical approach.
Modleski who clearly sees soap opera as a product of the patriarchal society, attempts to discover what is feminine about it. A significant element in her analysis is the emphasis on dialogue and a slow-paced narrative movement in soap opera, which, according to Modleski, is much more open to female ways of seeking pleasure than the classic film narrative with maximum action and minimum dialogue.[21]
She suggests that in soap opera climaxes are secondary (her psychoanalytical ap-

---

[18] Eva-Maria Warth, Ellen Seiter, Hans Borchers and Gabriele Kreutzner, Don't Treat Us Like We're Stupid and Naive: Towards an Ethnography of Soap Opera Viewers. In: Ellen Seiter et al., op. cit. p. 231.

[19] Dorothy Hobson, Soap Operas at Work. In: Ellen Seiter et al., op. cit.

[20] Charles Derry in: St.M. Kaminsky and J.H. Mahan (eds.), *American Television Genres*, (Chicago, 1985), pp. 85-86.

[21] Tania Modleski, The Search For Tomorrow in Today's Soap Opera. In: Tania Modleski, *Loving with A Vengeance: Mass Produced Fantasies for Women*, (Hamden, CT, 1982), p. 106.

proach suggests here an allusion to female sexuality) and any solution already bears the seed for new disorder.

Besides, the visual style of the soap opera with its numerous close-ups underlines intimacy. According to Modleski, it provides the spectator with training in "reading" other people, in being sensitive to their (unspoken) feelings at any given moment[22]. She suggests that the relation of the female viewer to the text is that of 'an ideal mother who watches her children' and "whose sympathy is large enough to encompass the conflicting claims of her family (she identifies with them all), and who has no demands or claims of her own (she identifies with no one character exclusively)".[23]

There is, however, one character which Modleski thinks is ambiguous. This is the soap opera villainess. On the one hand the spectator's anger is directed against her but on the other hand she acts out the spectator's fantasies of power. This ambiguity is enhanced by the Anglo/American soap opera's avoidance of final resolutions, so that the villainess is never finally punished.

Modleski's concept would need modification if applied to British soap operas where a clear distinction between villain/ess and good characters is not easily possible.

A further source of attraction for women is seen by Modleski in the close-knit community or extended family which soap opera is essentially about. She thinks that many women dream of a fully sufficient family or community, since in reality most of them find themselves at the centre of an isolated nuclear family.

All in all Modleski sees soap opera as a useful source of information for feminists on how a female aesthetic can operate. But since soap opera emerges from the patriarchal system, the ideas gained should be applied in the development of alternative narratives for women.

Modleski's study of the soap opera has fertilized a range of subsequent research. This is especially true of her notion that soap opera has the potential to subvert patriarchal values.

John Fiske draws on Modleski and other subsequent studies when he argues that the Anglo/American soap opera is only superficially about marriage and the family. The constant need for new story-lines in a continuous narrative is bound to create unstable marriages and disrupted families.[24]

The subversive potential of soap opera is further investigated by Mary Ellen Brown (1987) and Mary Ellen Brown and Linda Barwick (1989). Both treatises draw on qualitative research conducted among female viewers in the United States and Australia. Both articles stress the role of gossip in soap opera and about soap opera.

---

[22] ibid., p. 100.

[23] ibid., p. 92.

[24] John Fiske, *Television Culture*, (London and New York, 1987), p. 181.

Historically, Brown thinks (1987) that the soap opera is much more connected with a domestic oral tradition, such as "the handing down of recipes and lore about childbirth" than with the literary tradition of the domestic novel, to which it has become linked.[25]

According to Brown (1987), women are still frequently excluded from public discourse, which is largely held to be a male preserve. But women's private discourse is often depreciated as 'gossip'. Nevertheless, men have traditionally found female gossip threatening and have frequently associated it with witchcraft (Brown, 1987). Consequently, Brown and Barwick suggest that female gossip can be subversive of the patriarchal system and a source of female power.[26]

The soap opera as source and object of female gossip can therefore play a positive role in a group process, the result of which may be female empowerment, also in a politcal sense. This possibility is again attributed to the relative narrative openness of the endless soap opera text. For, it allows women to use the patriarchal myths which soap operas convey on the surface, for their own purposes[27]. Soap opera helps to "validate the value of a feminine culture which in masculine culture has been invalidated but not suppressed "[28].

So far there have been only few studies on the production of soap operas. The scarcity of such studies is due to the difficulties which researchers face to get access to studios.[29]

Michael Intintoli is an American anthropologist who was given access to the production of the now terminated Procter and Gamble/CBS soap opera *The Guiding Light* (on the air since 1937) and other serials.

He conceptualizes Soap Opera as a symbolic form and considers it as part of social structures and social processes.

His research methods were participient observation and open interviews.

The primary dynamic in the production of *The Guiding Light*, according to Intintoli, is the competition of *Procter and Gamble* for large demographically ideal audiences/markets of women between 18 and 49. Like Allen, Intintoli reflects on the changes in length and content of the soap opera, in order to attract additional segments of the audience. *Procter and Gamble* commissioned the administrative control and to a lesser degree the creative control to an advertising agency.

---

[25] Mary Ellen Brown, "The Politics of Soaps: Pleasure and Feminine Empowerment". *Australian Journal of Cultural Studies*, 4,2 (1987).

[26] Mary Ellen Brown and Linda Barwick, Motley Moments: Soap Opera, Carnival, Gossip and the Power of the Utterance. In: Mary Ellen Brown (ed.), *Television and Women's Culture*, (London, New Delhi, Newbury Park, CA, 1990).

[27] Mary Ellen Brown 1987, op. cit., p. 23.

[28] ibid.

[29] The restrictive policy of most television companies does not only result from enormously tight production schedules and the fear that story-line secrets may leak out but also from the fact that they try to maximise their profits by selling popular accounts on the productionwritten by producers or writers.

Compton Advertising hired the creative and production staff, while the technical staff was hired by CBS. The production process itself took place "in a hierarchically controlled organizational setting" which involved "an elaborate division of labor and the use of complex technologies to generate scenes, acts and episodes as part of the on-going storytelling".[30]

Intintoli concentrates on the investigation of six key roles in the production process: 1. supervision producer, 2. executive producer, 3. head writer, 4. performers, 5. directors, 6. line producers. One of Intintoli's findings is that Procter and Gamble's decision to diminish the power of the head writer in favour of the executive producer was a way for the company to consolidate its control over the programme in the face of fiercer competition from changed ABC soap operas.

---

[30] Michael James Intintoli, *Taking Soaps Seriously: The World of Guiding Light*, (New York, 1984), p. 121.

1.2.   The Purpose and Appproach of This Study

The purpose of this study is to investigate *Coronation Street* as a paradigm of the continuous serial, an international form of radio and television. It attempts to point out the ideosyncracy of the British serial and to assess its role as a model for other serials. The study looks at the cultural and institutional forces which shaped the serial in its early days. But it also approaches the serial as a narrative and dramatic continuum with specific rules and conventions and tries to elicit the internal and external mechanisms which have helped to sustain the programme for over thirty years in an increasingly competitive and diversified soap opera market. Finally, it tries to suggest ways in which viewers relate to the serial and make sense of it today.

The theoretical frame of this study is mainly derived from a combination of various structuralist/semiotic approaches. In the proposed tentative concept of the soap opera as an international television genre it draws on Claude Lévi-Strauss' myth analysis[31]. A central element in Lévi-Strauss' work is the thesis that the same basic structures operate in different cultural and social contexts. It is an underlying presupposition of this study that the same could be said of the structures and core conventions of the continuous serial.

In order to proceed from Lévi-Strauss' analysis of myth in primitive society to an analysis of the television discourse in industrialized society the study draws on the work of Umberto Eco, Roland Barthes and Christian Metz. Thoses authors share the assumption that film and television narratives, like myths or any other oral or written narrative, can be described as acts of speech operating according to a system of codes. Film and television, however, operate on a combination of various acoustic, linguistic and iconic codes. It is Barthes who, unlike Lévi-Strauss, stresses the mythological potential of Western culture in general and of the television discourse in particular.[32]

The study is particularly indebted to two academic books on soap opera with a semiotic perspective, which it tries to develop further in some of their key concepts. These books are the already summarized *Speaking of Soap Opera* by Robert Allen and the *Television Monograph: Coronation Street* by Richard Dyer et. al.. It places, for instance, Allen's definition of the core generic conventions of the US-American daytime serial and its antecendent, the radio serial, at the heart of a wider generic concept of the soap opera, which also embraces different cultural variations. Besides, it adopts Allen's concept of the continuous serial as a dynamic system which is changed by the forces of production interacting with the preferences of audiences in transition. From the collection of essays by Richard Dyer et al. published ten years ago, the book derives crucial insights into the cultural and

---

[31] Claude Lévi-Strauss, *The Naked Man: Indroduction to A Science of Mythology 4*, (New York, 1981).

[32] cf. Roland Barthes, *Mythologies*, (London, 1972), p. 109.

ideological forces which determined the specific narrative conventions of *Coronation Street*. However, it tries to extend those insights through investigating more recent developments in the serial and its production background and by applying some of its findings to other serials modelled on *Coronation Street*, notably the BBC1 serial *EastEnders* and the ARD[33] serial *Lindenstraße*.

The purpose of the close-analysis of two 1983 *Coronation Street* episodes in chapter V is to more explicitly prove some of the assumptions made earlier in the book and to provide a systematic analytical tool for the analysis of continuous serials in general. The shooting transcript which constitutes a fixation of the television discourse, is mainly based on Thomas Kuchenbuch's suggestions in *Einführung in die Filmanalyse* (1978) but it also draws on James Monaco's book *How to Read A Film* (1981). Especially, Monaco's representation of Christian Metz' concept of the *syntagm*, as the basic signifying unit in film is of importance.

Metz proposes eight types of syntagms in an increasing order of temporal and spatial complexity and distinguishes between chronological and a-chronological syntagms. The shooting transcript reflects that *Coronation Street* only consists of what in Metz' chart are the simplest syntagms, namely 'scene' and 'sequence'. Metz refers to them as 'linear narrative syntagms' and places them under the overall label of 'chronological syntagms'.[34]

---

[33] ARD is the first German public television channel.

[34] James Monaco on Christian Metz (pp. 188-189).

2. THE GENRE OF THE CONTINUOUS SERIAL

2.1. The Narrative Conventions

Horace Newcomb calls the soap opera "the furthest advanced television art" since it combines intimacy and continuity, two of the most important elements of the television aesthetic.[1]
To propose the concept of a 'soap opera genre' is not unproblematic. For, as with any concept of genre it is a system which has been worked out by researchers to group a range of texts or programmes. It is, however, a prominent feature of popular fiction, such as soap operas, that it synthesizes elements of other forms of fiction or documentary for popularity reasons. Matters are further complicated by the fact that viewers and also the professionals in the television industry may sometimes have different ideas of how certain televsion programmes ought to be grouped. Robert Allen points out that 'soap opera' is appropriated within at least three different discursive systems, namely that of the critical community, that of the industrial community and that of the viewer community.[2]
In addition, Allen suggests with only the Anglo/American countries in mind, that the concepts of what soap operas are, may vary from one country to another.

> "Finally, each country's experience with the range of texts to which the term 'soap opera' has been applied is different. It is a bit like ornithologist, taxidermists, and bird watchers from a dozen different countries all talking about birds, but in one country there are only eagles; in another pigeons and chickens but no eagles; in another macaws and pigeons but no eagles and chickens; and so on."[3]

Nevertheless, it is Allen who in *Speaking of Soap Operas*[4] defines the core textual elements and generic conventions of the soap opera. But he does this only in reference to the traditional North American daytime serials.
But apart from the daytime serials, the term soap opera is also applied to American prime time serials à la *Dallas* or *Dynasty* and to British Early prime time serials such as *Coronation Street*. In the article *Bursting Bubbles: Soap Opera, Audiences and The Limits of Genre* Allen proposes that a generic concept which embraces all those different types of continuous serials should be treated as tentative.

Despite that, it seems justified to develop the outlines of such a genre. For notwithstanding a number of variations, the term *soap opera* in Britain, North

---

[1] cf. Horace Newcomb, Toward a Television Aesthetic. In: Horace Newcomb (ed.), *Television: The Critical View*, (New York, Oxford, 1982).

[2] Robert C. Allen, Bursting Bubbles: Soap Opera, audiences and the limits of genre. In: Ellen Seiter et al. (eds.), *Remote Control: Television, Audiences and Cultural Power*, (London, New York, 1990), S. 45.

[3] ibid.

[4] cf. Robert Allen, *Speaking of Soap Operas*. (Chapel Hill, NC., 1985).

America and Australia invariably denotes a continuous programme, set in the present with open-ended episodes in which a number of different storylines alternate with eachother.

The *continuous serial* differs as far as its narrative structure - and presumably also as far as the psychological relation of the viewers to it are concerned, from a *drama series*. A series consists of a smaller or larger number of self-contained episodes.

Apart from the evening soap operas, such as *Dallas* for example, which are shown only once a week, soap operas in North America and Australia are normally broadcast five days a week for half an hour, 45 - or even 60 minutes during the day.

British soap operas have traditionally been shown less frequently, only two - sometimes three times a week. In 1989 the producers of *Coronation Street* increased the output of the serial from two - to three weekly episodes. The episodes of British soap operas so far last only half an hour during early prime time.

Another important characteristic of the Anglo/American soap opera is that, except for the evening soap operas, the fictional time is normally made to pass as closely as possible in accordance with the 'real' time of the viewers. According to Dennis Porter, the American daytime serials are marked by the "implicit claim to portray a parallel life."[5] Furthermore, he suggests that soap opera "offers itself to its audience as the representation of lives that are seperate from but continuous with their own."[6]

It is primarily the potential for endlessness which distinguishes a soap opera. But though quite a number of soap operas in North America and Britain have been shown continuously for decades, not every continuous serial is allowed 'to live out' its potential for endlessness. There have been many more serials which were started by television companies but were terminated after some time, since they did not attract a substantial enough share of the audience.

Monitoring the audience is a crucial factor in the production of a soap opera, even before its inception. In America it has been common for a considerable number of years to run a market research campaign before a soap opera is started, in order to elicit the preferences of the audience with regard to the serial in planning. In Britain this was done for the first time in 1984/85 with the BBC serial EastEnders. In a published review of the BBC Broadcasting Research Department it says:

> "It was at this very early stage, in January 1984 that the BBC's Broadcasting Research Department and the EastEnders production team began, what has turned out to be, a long period of researcher/producer co-operation."[7]

---

[5] Dennis Porter, Soap Time: Thoughts on A Commodity Art Form. In: Horace Newcomb, 1982, op. cit., p. 123.

[6] ibid.

[7] Vivien Marles and Nadine Nohr, *EastEnders*: The Research Contribution. In: *Annual Review of*

Thoughout its existence a soap opera is accompanied by regular audience surveys. The testing of audiences' responses to characters and storylines and the possibility that the producers may change planned plot lives because a majority of the audience seems to want it differently, renders the soap opera into an open text and imparts to it, as some researchers feel, a democratic quality.

That is why Allen thinks that the soap opera genre has to be conceptualized with an 'implicit' reader in mind. According to him, changing soap opera audiences and their changing attitudes had a share in transforming the genre.[8]

The openess of the soap opera narrative is further enhanced by a number of factors which, according to David Buckingham, stand between the 'text' and its recipients. Some such factors are the so-called 'spin-off' products (books, posters, calendars, records, T-shirts etc.) and the reports and speculations on stories and casts in special soap opera magazines (best known in the United States is *Soap Opera Digest*) and, particularly in Britain, the popular press. Buckingham is of the opinion that "these factors represent and mediate the programme in a variety of ways, and must therefore inevitably influence the processes by which viewers make sense of it".[9]

In comparison with other literary - or dramatic forms which consist of a beginning, a middle and an ending, the purpose of a soap opera "clearly is to never end and its beginning are always lost sight of (...) soap opera (...) is entirely composed of an indefinitely expandable middle."[10]

With some reservations, this still applies to American evening soap operas such as *Dallas* and *Dynasty*, which are broadcast in blocks of 26 episodes and only reappear after lengthy intervals.

Many Anglo/American soap operas have been continued for decades. Even *Dallas* up to now has lasted for fourteen years.

Peter Buckman illustrates the ideosyncracy of the endless soap opera narrative by referring to the American radio soap operas, the direct antecendents of the daytime serials on television. The last of those radio serials were stopped around 1960 but more or less open-ended.[11] According to Christine Geraghty, the same happened to the British radio serial *Waggoner's Walk*, which was stopped in 1980.

Geraghty suggests:
"Indeed, the writers seem to have humorously recognised that a serial - even in this situation - has a future, by finishing the serial with a

---

BBC Broadcasting Research Findings Nr. 12 (London, 1986), p. 69.

[8] cf. Robert Allen, 1985, op. cit.

[9] David Buckingham, *Public Secrets: EastEnders and Its Audience*, (London, 1987), p. 152.

[10] Dennis Porter in: Horace Newcomb (ed.), Television: The Critical View, (New York, Oxford, 1982) p. 124.

[11] cf. Peter Buckman, *All For Love: A Study in Soap Opera*, (London, 1984), p. 34.

proposal of marriage which the woman concerned asks for time to think about. 'Of course', comes the reply, 'you have all the time in the world', (...) One is left with a sense that the serial has not stopped but is still taking place, an extreme case of 'unchronicled growth' "[12]

The endlessness of the Anglo/American soap opera distinguishes it from its Latin American counterpart, the telenovela, another variation of the long-running continuous serial. Unlike the soap opera, the telenovela is expected to have a happy-ending at some stage. Most telenovelas consist of 150 to 250 episodes, which are broadcast five days a week over periods of six to nine months continuously, though some very successful telenovelas have been extended to last for more than a year. Unlike the Anglo/American soap opera, the telenovela has, one central plot which runs from the beginning to the end. Although the central plot is entangled with a great number of subplots, the narrative structure of the telenovela is strictly speaking linear and not spiral, as is sometimes suggested for the soap opera.[13] But both, the soap opera and the telenovela, work on the basis of a system of fragmentation and delay.

But because of the absence of a central plot which stretches through the whole serial in the Anglo/American soap opera, several narrative strands are given approximately an equal length of time in each episode.
Usually, each episode consists of two, three or even more little plots.
Exceptions are made when an episode deals with extraordinary events such as for example weddings, severe marital crises, major accidents or characters' disappearance or death, or, as it has been the case in *Coronation Street,* a strike.

There is rarely a final solution of any one problem in the Anglo/American soap opera, but rather temporary solutions always tend to engender new problems and new storylines.

Nevertheless, Christine Geraghty stresses that the soap opera form, despite its endlessnes, relies on moments of temporary resolution. According to her, this is to achieve a certain equilibrium within the form and also to allow the audience some temporary respite from the endless pattern of open problems. Geraghty suggests furthermore that each serial generally has its own distinctive modes to develop short-term situations of harmony, but often this is achieved by one storyline being ended with the whole serial community involved, for once all quarrels and differences forgotten. Other stories are temporarily suppressed, though they may be taken up again in the next episode.[14]

---

[12] Christine Geraghty, "The Continuous Serial - A Definition", in: Richard Dyer et al., *Television Monograph: Coronation Street* (London, BFl, 1981), p. 11.

[13] Tania Modleski suggests that the soap opera form could be a possible 'germ-cell' for a feminist form of narrative. Since she sees the spiral narrative in soap opera as antithetic to the classic linear (male) film narrative. cf. Tania Modlevski, "The Search for Tomorrow in Today's Soap Operas". *Film Quarterly* (Autumn 1979).

[14] Christine Geraghty, The Continuous Serial - A Definition. In: Richard Dyer et al. (1981), p. 15.

But even weddings, which in the telenovela like in other types of romance often constitute the final happy ending by which a central conflict is terminated, are in the Anglo/American soap opera only temporary points of resolution. Although they are definitely highlights, after all many plots centre upon courting, they only give rise to new storylines, such as in due time stories about marital crises, child bearing or a bossy mother-in-law.

Death is probably the most final resolution which a continuous serial can provide; yet, even then stories can arise, for example, from some late discovery of the deceased person's doings. But death in a mystified way also contributes to some serials' sense of the past. For, the departed person is likely to be referred to now and again by the others. In *Coronation Street* the photos of dead members of the 'street' are sometimes focused on by the camera, often as a source of support for distressed relatives.

In addition to the short-term plots, no continuous serial can do without a certain number of more long-term plots built on continuing problems which remain unsolved and run through the narrative patterns of a serial for a lengthy period. Such longterm problems may create an extra impetus for regular viewers to continue watching the serial. To the irregular viewer, however, they impart the feeling of not having missed too much, since it is easy to recapture the long-term, slowly advancing storyline.

In some sense, they can also be labelled long-term 'cliffhangers', sometimes barely visible but growing stronger at other times.

Occasionally a cliffhanger is also created through the sort of knowledge which is given to the audience. One possibility is to keep the audience in the dark over a particular problem to make them watch the subsequent episode for more information. Another possibility, however, is, to let the audience know more than most of the characters in the serial ostensibly know. In that case the audience is given the impetus to continue watching the programme to see it all revealed sometime.

As will be explained in the next section, the term 'cliffhanger' is originally derived from the early American cinema where it was first employed as a dramatical device in silent film serials. However, with soap opera, the term 'cliffhanger' is mostly used for the more immediate cliffhangers at the end of each individual episodes. In that context 'cliffhanger' means a moment of tension or emotional intensity by which an episode is terminated in order to arouse the curiosity of the viewers. The 'cliffhanger' is a narrative device which the Anlo/American soap opera and the Latin American telenovela share.

The different stories of a soap opera episode are usually only loosely linked, either on the visual level by filmic devices or through strategies in the organisation of the narrative. One such strategy is that two stories reflect on eachother by focussing upon the same motif, only presented in different contexts. According to Christine Geraghty, in *Coronation Street* serious stories are parodied by comic ones.[15]

A further narrative device by which the different strands of one episode are linked, is the use of gossip. Characters involved in one plot gossip about events or characters of another plot. The narrative role of gossip is brought about by the general dominance of dialogue over action in soap opera.

The latter feature of the soap opera narrative has developed because of budgetary constraints, which have traditionally been administered in the production of soap operas. Instead of showing the action, soap opera has characters who comment on it.

Despite the fact that evening soap operas such as *Dallas* and *Dynasty* produced on much larger budgets than the daytime serials, they have also adopted the primacy of dialogue as a convention.

Soap opera storylines almost invariably centre around human interest stories rooted in the lives of individual characters, rather than major political or social issues. The backbone of any soap opera are personal relationships, which predominate even in serials that are set in places of work, such as offices or hospitals.

As has already been said, Robert Allen distiguishes between three major types of relationships: "kinship, romance and social" and suggests: "Much of the appeal of soap operas resides in the complexity and overlap among these categories of actual and potential relationships for any particular character."[16]

Embedded into the personalized relational code of the soap opera are to a varying degree also themes which belong to such categories as crime, social-, political - or medical problems. Thus, in recent years the problem of AIDS has been treated in a number of soap operas, including the British serial *EastEnders* and the German serial *Lindenstraße*. Such problems can, however, only be dealt with in soap opera if they can be related to one of the regular characters or if it is possible to introduce a new character into the soap opera community or extended family. Normally, it is also a convention of the soap opera form that problems are solved within the serial community and not by forces from the outside, except fate.

The serial communities in the American daytime serials, Australian and British soap operas consist of people who live in the same neighbourhood or work together in one place (eg. hospital, law firms, hotels etc.) whereas the American evening soap operas (like the Latin American telenovelas) seem to rely more on large extended families.

It is, however, a common feature of all long-runnig continuous serials in the Anglo/American format (in contrast to the Latin American format) that the nuclear families are by narrative convention (trough the need for new storylines) rather fragile. With reference to *Coronation Street* Marion Jordan infers:

> "Much of the skill of the programme (and of the success of the genre) can be seen in the way in which it omits what is sociologically the normative grouping of mother, father, two children, while still managing to

---

[15] Christine Geraghty, op. cit., p. 12.

[16] cf. Robert Allen, 1985, op. cit., p. 74.

assert that it is about just such groups. It is difficult to think of children with two parents on the spot recently."[17]

It seems to be a general rule of the continuous serial that unmarried characters offer more potential for plots, "marriage easily diminishes a character".[18] As has already been said, here clearly lies a contradiction in the conventions of the continuous serial for on the one hand love and marriage are centrepieces of the serials, whereas on the other hand, the constant demand for new storylines means that the 'estate of holy matrimony' cannot be too permanent.

> "In a sense, the conventions of the genre are such that the normal order of things in *Coronation Street* is precisely that of broken marriages, temporary liaisons, availability for 'lasting' romantic love which in fact never lasts. This order, the reverse of the patriarchal norm, is in a sense interrupted by the marriages and happy family interludes, rather than vice versa."[19]

As action is scarce on soap opera and dialogue prominent, the soap opera stands and falls with its characters. Continuity, for instance, is perhaps to a greater extent achieved through continuity of character than through the technique of plot construction. All serials rely on the regular appearance of a core of longstanding characters, who may become as familiar to the consistent viewer as his/her next door neighbours.

In the long run, it is inevitable that the original cast is gradually replaced by new characters. *Coronation Street* features at present only one character - Ken Barlow - who has been on the cast ever since the programme started. However, there are others who have been on the cast for ten, fifteen or twenty years.

Often it is not easy to choose the right time and way to get rid of a long-standing character without causing too much public outcry and a consequent drop in a serial's popularity chart. But, since in the American daytime serials and British serials none of the characters is so central to the narrative that it could not continue without him/her, any character could be written out. This, however, is not so easily done in the American prime time serials, which are built on the centrality of characters such as J.R. or Alexis.

Each serial has a range of established serial types, moulds in which new members of the cast, even if they are given a different identy, have to fit, unless serial makers are willing to introduce new character types. Peter Buckman seems to think that all serials basically rely on the same raw types, whereas Christine Geraghty suggests that different types should rather be defined from a point of reference within the respective serial.

Buckman lists the following types which, however, seem to apply more to American soap operas than to British serials: a.) the decent husband, b.) the bitch (according to him, not a character who features as prominently on British serials

---

[17] Marion Jordan, Realism and Convention, in: Richard Dyer et al. op. cit, p. 32.

[18] *Teaching Coronation Street*, (London BFI, 1983), p. 63.

[19] *Teaching Coronation Street*, (London BFI, 1983), p. 63.

as on American ones), c.) the good woman (or devoted wife), d.) the king/queen figure, e.) the romantic hero, f.) the innocent heroine and g.) the ruthless villain.

With mainly the British serial *Coronation Street* in mind, Geraghty uses a three-dimensional approach to define characterisation in continuous serials. First, she considers each character as an individuated character who is marked by certain traits which are presented as uniquely his or her own.

Secondly, Geraghty sees characters also as serial types but in a somewhat different way from Buckman. For *Coronation Street* she defines, for instance, an 'Elsie Tanner type' who is sexy, rather tartly dressed, hot-tempered and impulsive. Other female characters in the serial can then be described as either belonging also to the 'Elsie Tanner type, as having some features of that type or as being completely different from Elsie like Mavis Riley, for instance. Mavis Riley could herself be the model for a spinsterly type of woman. A similar typology could be found for the male characters of a serial. Geraghty's third category is the character's status position.

"(...) by this, I am referring to the position they occupy in the serial in terms crucially of sex, age and marital position and sometimes in terms of class and work."[20]

According to her, the combination of qualities from the above mentioned three categories determine the range of plots for which characters are available. For, while plots which centre upon more general problems might be suitable for almost all characters, other plots, such as marriage or childbirth, can only employ certain characters.

As to the way in which the characteristics of the people in soap operas are conveyed to the viewer, Christine Geraghty points out:

"Because the serial has to be comprehensible to both the committed follower and the casual viewer, and given the number of characters involved, characterisation has to be swift and sharp; the immidiate sense of what a character is and what roles/he is likely to play has to be given quickly, using such elements as clothes and voice."[21]

In *Coronation Street* it sometimes seems to be the case that the idiosyncracies of one character are revealed only when this character is juxtaposed with another. Stan and Hilda Ogden were good examples of that convention. (Apparently that was the reason why their marriage was presented as being so permanent). Before Stan's death in 1984 Hilda was invariably presented as a nagging wife with only an occasional soft spot for her husband. After Stan's death, however, she was turned into a considerate and caring grandmother.

In their need for swift and sharp characterisation serial-makers can hardly avoid drawing on stereotypes. Nevertheless, characters sometimes act contrary to what is expected of them, which Christine Geraghty conceives as an element of self-reflec-

---

[20] Christine Geraghty, op. cit., p. 20.

[21] Christine Geraghty, op. cit., p. 19.

tion in the serials.

Tania Modleski indicates that in American serials there often exists a tendency to polarise characters; the heroine, for instance, a good woman who accepts personal suffering without questioning is set against a villainess, a bad woman, a manipulating mother who inflicts suffering rather than suffers herself.[22] Even though Marilyn Matelski suggests that in recent years characterisation on the American daytime serials (not the prime time serials) has become more-dimensional, it is correct to maintain that characters in the British serials are much less polarised.

As far as *Coronation Street* is concerned, individual stories may rely on the antagonistic behaviour of two characters, but the line between 'good' and 'evil' is not clearly drawn.

Even Ena Sharples, who quit the serial in the late seventies but has become a legendary character with all her sharp edges that left little room for amiability, could not be grouped as a bad character. Her harshness did not remain unexplained; the viewers now and again were reminded that she had had a hard life working in the mills from an early age on. Moreover, she also had her good sides, for instance, a somewhat shrewd devotion to the street community.

In the same way in which there is no real villain or villainess in *Coronation Street,* there is no undisputably good character, either.

Ken Barlow has always been presented "as an eminently respectable dogooder."[23] But despite his respectability which in recent year has made him appear quite pompous, he has had several love-affairs and on some occasions has acted very opportunistically.

Most novels and plays present one or several main characters whose development is depicted in a finite narrative or drama. In the so-called 'community serials' such as *Coronation Street,* however, there are a whole range of characters who are all of the same category; in one sense they are all main characters, in another sense they all appear flat and more like minor characters in a novel. If a comparison between Dickens' characters and the characters in *Coronation Street,* which is so often suggested, is at all possible, it can only concern Dickens' minor characters. If a Mr. Micawber, a Mr. Bumble, a Mrs. Gargery rather than David Copperfield or Pip, could be imagined appearing continuously for several decades, they would probably resemble the characters in *Coronation Street.*

As far as style is concerned, Geraghty thinks that:

> "It is possible for a serial to cover a wide range of stories and styles without disturbing the serial format by playing them against very familiar elements - the signature tune, the setting, long-standing characters."[24]

---

[22] cf. Tania Modleski, The Search For Tommorrow in Today's Soap Opera. In: T. Modleski, Loving with A Vengeance: Mass Produced Fantasies for Women, (Hamden, CT, 1982).

[23] ibid. p. 75.

[24] ibid., p. 12.

Allen infers that in the American Daytime serials writers in their constant search for new storylines have based plots on "popular movies, novels, other television programs, press reportage of the Mafia, religious cults, and terrorism, among other topics."[25] But he also stresses that all those elements were absorbed by the basic structure of the slow-moving soap opera narrative, relying on the above-mentioned three categories of personal relationships, and the Realism (especially Realism of time) which marks the Anglo/American soap opera.[26]

2.2.   Dramatic and Filmic Conventions

Any exploration of the characteristics of the continuous TV serial would remain incomplete without consideration of the non-verbal, non-literary conventions of vision and sound.

As far as sound in British soap operas is concerned, the concept of Realism in that country has so far implied that sound, apart from the signature tunes, can only come from 'natural' sources, like music from a radio, from a musical instrument or a song sung by one of the characters, whereas in American serials, sound - especially music - is used as a commentative element.

Due to production constraints, it has become part of the conventions of soap opera that most scenes are set in closed rooms with a table, a bar, a counter etc. in the centre. People either sit or stand and spend most of the time talking. Whereas location shots are traditionally rare in soap operas, though they have become more frequent in *Coronation Street* and other British serials in recent years.

The latter tendency can most probably be attributed to the competition with the American prime time serials, such as *Dallas* and *Dynasty*. Since those were - and are produced on much larger budgets they had more outside scenes, which partially take the viewer in exotic places.

Subsequently, other long-running continuous serials have gradually increased their amount of location shots and occasionally even transfer some of their characters to distant holiday resorts. Thus, *Coronation Street* character Bet Lynch in 1987 eloped to Spain and business partner and husband in spe Alec Gilroy followed her to Torremolinos. Before, such trips untertaken by *Coronation Street* characters (eg. Elsie Tanner's journey to Portugal) were only talked about in the serial but not actually shown. The German serial *Lindenstraße* included several sequences filmed in Greece and in more recent years some of the characters travelled to France.

Described in Christian Metz' terminology soap opera is marked by the absence of a-chronological syntagms. For the most part it consists of syntagms that are chronological and linear (unity of time, place and action), which remind more

---

[25] Rober Allen, 1985, op. cit., p. 87.

[26] In contrast to the Latin American telenovela which employs historical and contemporary settings, the Anglo/American soap opera is invariably set in the present and the fictional time is largely identical with the 'here and now' of the spectators.

of a stage play than a complex film narrative.

Consequently, transitions from one sequence to the next, which usually also involve a switch over to a different setting and a different storyline,[27] are not smooth but appear stagey. Often sequences are linked through key-words in the dialogue or visual clues which occur in one sequence and are then reestablished in the following one: for example, the last shot of one sequence focuses on a door and the first shot of the next sequence also focuses on a door. Since the respective doors belong to different narrative contexts, two plots are thus linked. Bernhard Timberg points out that at the end of each sequence of soap opera, "Images congeal into fixed tableaux".[28]

The duration of shots in soap opera is on average rather long and camera movements are generally scarce or very slow. Richard Paterson suggests with regard to *Coronation Street*.

> "Sometimes a developing shot is used with the camera panning to follow the action. In an early episode there is a tracking shot, though this is never used in current production."[29]

Shots become considerably shorter if shown in quick shot-reverse-shot patterns in situations of tension. In *Coronation Street* shots are also more numerous and on the whole shorter in the 'Rover's Return', "the main place of exchange in the *Street*".[30]

As for the transition between shots within sequences, Richard Paterson suggests that in *Coronation Street* "the cutting between shots is almost invariably motivated by dialogue.[31]

In line with the overall narrative organisation of soap opera, the camera style is determined by the centrality of character. That is one reason - the small sets are another - why 'extreme long' or 'long' shots which would depict characters in the middle of a landscape do not occur frequently in soap operas. 'Establishing' shots are used at the beginning or end of an episode, sometimes also at the beginning or end of scenes within an episode. Occasionally, it is a 'full' shot which is used to portray a character in his or her full length, but most of the time soap opera depicts its characters in shots that vary between 'medium', 'close-up' and 'detail' shots.

The frequent 'close-up' shots contribute to the "intimacy" which Horace Newcomb

---

[27] With regard to *Coronation Street*, Richard Paterson and John Stewart infer that the different plots are not only distinguished by themes and the characters involved but frequently also by different settings, according to the motto "every front door hides a story". Cf. Richard Paterson and John Stewart, Street Life. In: Richard Dyer et al., 1981, op. cit., p. 86.

[28] Bernard Timberg, The Rhetoric of Camera in Television Soap Opera. In: Horace Newcomb (ed.), *Television: The Critical View,* (New York, Oxford, 3rd ed. 1982), pp. 132-147, p. 145.

[29] Richard Paterson, The Production Context of *Coronation Street*. In: Richard Dyer et al., op. cit., pp. 64-65.

[30] Richard Paterson, op. cit., p. 64.

[31] Richard Paterson, The Production Context of *Coronation Sreet*. In: Richard Dyer et al., op. cit., p. 65.

sees as an aesthetic characteristic of soap opera. Bernhard Timberg suggests. "(...)
This close-up camera style has the effect of bringing the viewer closer and closer
to the hidden emotional secrets soap opera explores (...)."[32]
Another characteristic of the soap opera style of camera is its almost invariable
use of the eye-level angle.
Extremely low or high camera angles are employed only in extraordinary situations.
It is sometimes suggested that soap opera is especially prone to engage its viewers
in a para-social interaction, and indeed many of its characteristic features seem to
be geared to evoking as close a relationship with the characters as possible. The
soap opera convention of grouping characters mostly in open groups of two or
three further sustains the impression. For, it offers to the viewer the opportunity to
imagine him/herself part of that group and thus part of the 'soap world'. Bernard
Timberg stresses:

> "Soap Opera is built on twos and threes. Its basic structure rests on
> two- generally two characters engaged in intimate dialogue. (...) Some-
> times a third person will enter the scene via doorbell, door knock, tele-
> phone call, or simply by walking into the room."[33]

Very often scenes revolve around a missing other character and the viewer
may slip into the role of the one who is absent.
According to Timberg characters in soap-opera frames are often grouped in half-
circles or in z-axis alignments. The latter means that one character is in the fore-
ground while another is set deeper in the background, forming a z-axis, with the
camera relating the two, which often involves over-the-shoulder shots.
Another technique frequently used to portray two -, or two characters plus a third
one engaged in a conversation or a row is the shot/reverse shot pattern.

Since action in soap opera is rather slow and often even minute, "hand, face,
body gestures and intonation take on emblematic significance (...)."[34] Objects can
also become emblems or symbols.
This can be exemplified by to 1980 episodes of *Coronation Street* which deal with
one character's (Emily Bishop) discovery that her second husband Arnold Swain is
a bigamist. In those episodes the wedding ring on Emily's hand is focused on by
the camera as an emblem of her marriage. Likewise, a tray of fruits and a vase of
tastefully arranged flowers are suggested as emblems of Emily's characteristic
sense of order and harmony. In the course of the two episodes, however, the ab-
andoned marriage ring and the fading flowers become symbols of the deteriorating marital relationship.
Since the visual codes of *Coronation Street* reflect a Realist or in some respects
even Naturalist approach. The emblematic or metonymic use of objects is more

---

[32] Bernhard Timberg, op. cit., p. 135.

[33] Bernhard Timberg, op. cit., p. 142.

[34] Bernhard Timberg, op. cit., p. 138.

common than their use as symbols.

2.3. The History and Evolution of The Soap Opera

Peter Buckman refers to the "sub-culture" of the continuous serial that has flourished for half a century"[35], insinuating that the form of the continuous serial started with the American radio soap operas of the 1930s.
Nevertheless, the serial form as such with its established character formulae has been a characteristic of popular fiction and drama for many centuries. Louis James suggest:

> "The popular imagination (...) is interested in character conceived on a simple, well-defined plane, which exists independent of a complex literary form. All the popular heroes have been subject to prolonged story cycles, whether Odysseus, King Athur, Sexton Blake, or the Archers, the successful English radio serial."[36]

The technical innovations of the 19th century added a new industrial and highly commercial element, which henceforth was to determine the production of popular fiction serials in the print- and the electronic media [37]. In a number of countries, serialized stories and novels (in newspapers, magazines or distributed by 'colportage') were ravishingly absorbed by the newly emerging mass readership of the 19th century. That is why a great number of writers tried to earn their livlihood by wrting fiction serials.
Prominent examples in France were the *feuilletons* (novels written directly for the press)[38] by authors like Eugén Sue. In Britain and the United States many people waited impatiently for the next instalment of the novels of Charles Dickens or others.
Dickens achieved enormous success through publishing his novels in inexpensive monthly or weekly instalments or by serializing them in periodicals.

Dickens' literary characters can be defined as stock characters of the literary period in which he created his work. Nevertheless, many of them appeared so realistic, or were at least so close to what the imagination of the public demanded to identify with a character that their fictionality became blurred. Early in Dickens's

---

[35] Peter Buckman, *All For Love: A Study in Soap Opera*, (London, 1984), p.76.

[36] Louis James, *Fiction For The Working Man 1830-1850*, (London, 1963), p. 7.

[37] c.f. for example Louis James, op. cit.

[38] Originally *feuilleton* in French or *folitin* in Spanish meant *chapbook* (serialized stories which were distributed through colportage, mostly in issues of eight or 16 pages). In Spain and Latin America there also exists the term *cordèl*, since those pieces of popular literature were often bound together by a string. Today *feuilleton* is also used to refer to a popular television serial with open-ended episodes (in contrast to *a serie* with self-contained episodes).
The style of the 19th century French feuilleton and the Spanish folletìn still inform the contemporary Latin American telenovela.

career, for instance, the characters of *The Pickwick Papers* (1836) became the centre of a veritable cult. Then eventually became some sort of communal property and they were able to function outside of the narrative frame they were originally conceived in. That is to say a spate of plagiarisms emerged which preyed upon Dickens original (e.g. *The Penny Pickwick, Oliver Twiss* etc.) Another famous example which testifies the capacity of convincing fictional characters to cross the borderline between a fictional world and reality is Conan Doyle's Sherlock Holmes. The 'master detective' was so popular that it evoked a public outcry when the author made known his plan to stop the series. This is not so very different from what happens in the popular press in Britain today when a long-established character in a serial is doomed to be written out of the programme or even the whole serial is to be stopped. Likewise, people in the 19th century addressed letters to Sherlock Holmes' fictional domicile in Baker Street, as people today write to 'Coronation Street' to contact the fictional inhabitants.

The mechanical innovations in the printing industry after 1830 (e.g. the invention of the steam press) and a new quality of entrepreneurial spirit among publishers accelerated the publication of penny issue novels or periodicals garnished with illustrations for all levels of taste.

For the printer/publisher of that time serial publications had the advantage that they could be printed with almost no capital, "since the income of the one issue paid for the printing of the next".[39] Louis James infers that in some branches of the production system of popular or pulp literature, publishers already imposed standardized modes of writing, which suggest a resemblance to the way in which the scripts of soap operas are written.

Louis James gives the following example:

> "Edward Lloyd showed early the practical ingenuity which accounted for much of his success. When a writer was established as a reliable contributor, Lloyd issued him with specially lined paper, which covered with average-sized writing, would constitute one penny issue. Payment was strictly on delivery, ten shillings a number. (...) The pace, however, was inexorable, (...) The method of payment naturally influenced the style of these romances. (...) authors wrote as much conversation as possible, and made their lines very short; (...)[40]

According to Raymond William Stedman (the authoritative historian of the American serial in all its forms) there is a 19th century genre of fiction which is more directly linked to the evolution of the radio - and television soap opera than perhaps the works of Dickens. The genre he is referring to is the Domestic Novel (written for example by such authors as Augusta Evans Wilson or Mary Jane Holmes).

But Stedman also sees an indirect link to the silent-film chapter plays that emerged even before the radio soap opera. Stedman suggests three main aspects

---

[39] Louis James, *Fiction For The Working Man 1830-1850*, (London, (1963), p. 8.

[40] Louis James, op. cit., p. 33.

which the domestic novels shared with the early radio soap operas. First, domestic novels were frequently issued in instalments and appeared in so called 'story papers'. Secondly, they were primarily intended for women, hence they focused on heroines rather than heroes. Thirdly,

> "they were set in the present, with most of the action occuring in the home. While subjects were commonplace, the plots were filled with strange diseases, lost mates, deserted wives and marriages in name only. Current events received no more attention than they did in radio serials (...)"[41]

Like the subsequent radio - and television serials, the domestic novels were marked more by a melodramatic - than a comic tone, "the emphasis was upon suffering". As in the radio serials action was scarce and mystery and suspense plot did not play an important role. "The domestic novel was concerned with duties and decisions, not events. Nevertheless, countless episodes were employed to tell the meandering story."[42]

Another less direct influence in the United States were the *film chapter-plays*, which were invented by newspaper-owners as promotional tools.
In 1912 the editor of the monthly American magazine *The Ladies World* was the first who had the Edison Kinescope Company produce a silent film version of each episode of the story *What Happened To Mary?*, which the magazine serialized at the same time.
The two ventures poved to be mutually supporting. Subsequently, a number of other American magazine and newspapers followed, though a few years later the chapter-plays could well survive financially without that firm link to the hot-house of the American press.

Like the domestic novels, the film chapter-plays up to the middle of the 1920s centred upon heroines rather than male heroes, (only gradually did they become more male oriented). Stedman infers that

> "The early serial era was established upon the heroines, of course. As they would a few decades later in soap opera, male stars often had to operate in feminine shadow, providing rescues when needed and reacting to situations created by the struggle between villain and leading lady."[43]

But unlike the domestic novels and the forthcoming radio soap operas, those film serials were not predominantly set in the home. Rather, they were blends of romance, action and suspense drama. Often the heroines even had to perform quite neck-breaking scenes. Frequently, episodes ended in dangerous situations, leaving the spectators' suspense or thrill unrelieved until the subsequent episode.

---

[41] Raymond William Stedman, *The Serials* (Norman, 1971), p. 286.

[42] Raymond William Stedman, *The Serials* (Norman, 1971), p. 289.

[43] Raymond William Stedman, *The Serials* p. 38.

Hence the name 'cliffhanger'.

While in Briain the first Director-General of BBC radio, John Reith, was very much opposed to soap operas, the commercial radio stations in the United States were all too keen to use the form of the continuous serial. For, already in the 1930s American radio was governed by market forces and there was fierce competition for listeners and advertising money. The continuous day-time serial became a favourite tool in that commercial struggle, an instrument which was predominantly geared to attract housewives, the main buyers of consumer goods. Soon the systems developed in such a way that the radio networks only sold transmission time to sponsors or advertising agencies, who made there own serials to go with their commercials. Procter and Gamble, the long established soap and cooking oil conglomerate, were among the first to advertise on radio and also the most willing sponsor of serials (according to Peter Buckman, the company had 22 serials under its sponsorship in 1939, worth 8 3/4 million Dollars. It thus is not too surprising that the form was nicknamed 'soap opera'. Robert Allen infers:

> "With increasing amounts of advertising needed to maintain sales levels and market shares of its products in the first years of the Depression, Procter and Gamble instituted an unparalleled program of market research to assure that its advertising budget was spent as efficiently as possible. (...) Procter and Gamble saw the opportunity of creating favorable associations between entertaining programming heard while the listener performed household tasks and the Procter and Gamble products that could be used in their accomplishment." [44]

Procter and Gamble still sponsor five TV soap operas, though continuous sponsorship of soap operas is no longer very common, most soap operas in America are today owned by the networks.

The first Procter and Gamble soap opera which proved successful in 1933 was *Ma Perkins* designed as advertising vehicle for the washing-powder Oxydol. The serial was introduced by the male narrator as follows:

> "And here's Oxydol's own Ma Perkins again. The true-life story of a woman whose life is the same, (...) whose problems are the same as those of thousands of other women in the world today. A woman who has spent all her live taking care of her home: washing and cooking and cleaning and raising her family. And now her husband's death has pitched her head-foremost into being the head of her family as well as the mother. And we'll hear her true-life story every day at this time (...).
> Before we hear from Ma Perkins today, though, I want to tell you about something else for a minute that will be of vital interest to every housewife listening; about a remarkable new laundry-soap discovery that (...)"[45]

---

[44] Robert Allen, 1985, op. cit., p. 115.

[45] ibid., p. 115/116.

To guarantee the incessant flow of ideas and stories for the numerous serials demanded, personalities like Frank and Anne Hummert, Irna Phillips and Gertrude Berg were needed. In order to maximize their own profit and that of the advertising agencies, they managed to rationalize the process of writing fiction to an extent never seen before.

"Having realized that one serial idea was not going to make them and the agency rich, they organized themselves into a machine for the production of plot ideas. Their working method was a streamlined version of agency practive. The Hummerts dreamed up the story (...) They sold the idea to a sponsor (...)"[46]

Sponsors naturally had the right to interfere with the content of a serial.

"Once a sponsor was signed up, the Hummerts would outline each episode in some detail, to make sure it conformed to the sponsor's expectations. Then they would hand over the drudgery of actually writing the words the characters were to speak to dialoguers. The Hummerts thus kept total control of characters and plot - and incidentally of the rights in each serial".[47]

The influence of the domestic novel affected that a domestic setting with often a mother figure at the centre and elements of romance and melodrama became staple devices of the radio serials, whereas comical elements did only rarely play an important part.
However, already then the most striking feature of most radio soap operas was their longevity. Not seldom were those early US-American radio soap operas broadcast for more than ten years, some even for twenty years.
Around 1960, however, the radio audience declined in favour of television and sponsors in America gradually lost interest in radio soap operas. By 1960 the last six radio serials were brought to an end, despite massive protests from listeners. Some of the radio serials were taken over into television.

Incidentally, the predecessors of the Latin American telenovela the radionovela were initiated in the 1940s by the same US-American conglomerates - mainly producers of soap, detergents, toothpaste and other household goods - which had started the North American radio soap opera in the thirties. Expanding via Cuba to other countries of the Latin American subcontinent, they also spread the radionovela.
One of the earliest radionovelas made in Cuba but taken over by a number of other Latin American countries and later made into several television versions, was *El Derecho de Nacer* (1946). But already then the two types of continuous serials differed considerably in length, with the US-American radio soap opera being broadcast for much longer.

---

[46] Robert Allen, 1985, op. cit., p. 10.

[47] ibid.

In 1952 the serial *The Guiding Light* became the first successful television soap opera in the United States. The serial had been on the radio for more than a decade before it was transferred to television and for four year it was broadcast on both media. According to the television historian Erik Barnouw, the final breakthrough of the soap opera on television only occured several years later, after the daily episodes had been extended from the traditional 15 minutes to 30 minutes.

Through an analysis of the scripts of the early television soap operas, Robert Allen found out that the prolongation of the episodes and the visual dimension of the television medium affected structural changes in the serials. Instead of only one or two narrative strands, the television serials now had three to four. Another change was the disappearence of the narrator who, as in the example of *Ma Perkins* cited above, had introduced 'the current state of events' in the serial and brought over the 'commercial message'. In the television serials the viewers were now directly confronted with the narrative events and the advertisements were inserted as commercials.

Although differing considerably in technique from radio, television continued to employ the same formula: open-ended stories on the domestic concerns, daily hopes and despairs of more or less average middle class families, living in small towns or suburbs. Up to the present day most of the day-time television soap operas resemble televised radio programmes more than films. For, visualization is minimal, action scarce and dialogues dominant.

As has already been indicated, there occured over the years a number of shifts and variations in character and style in the Anglo/American soap opera which sometimes resulted in the establishment of distinct types.

One such variation, which occured already in the fifties, is the evolution of the medical soap opera set in a hospital or a doctor's surgery. Classical examples are the American *General Hospital* and the British *Emergency Ward Ten* (1957 to 1966). In recent years Australia has produced and exported quite a number of soap operas set in doctor's surgeries.

As another example of a more recent shift in the soap opera genre, the increasing use of crime elements could be cited. Nevertheless, already *The Edge of the Night*, which started in the 1950s but was still on in the 1980s carried a lot of crime. According to Peter Buckman it is the nearest the genre comes to a thriller.[48]

A shift towards the employment of younger characters and their problems ocurred with the aim to capture teenage audiences.

But the most significant variation in the genre has been the invention of the prime-time soap operas *Dallas* and *Dynasty* in the late seventies. In order to attract also a greater share of male viewers to the genre, the form was ultered in such a way that there was more emphasis on prominent male characters than in the day-time serials. Besides, the settings were shifted from the world of the suburban middle-class family to the glamourous society of Texas oil barons with their fast cars and expensive life-styles. In addition, quite a number of thriller - and Western

---

[48] Robert Allen, 1985, op. cit., p. 32.

elements were included. Due to higher production budgets there is significantly more concern for visualization.

Muriel Cantor and Suzanne Pingree think that the prime time serials are too different to be grouped under the label *soap opera*.[49] The reasons they give are that with blocks of 26 - and only one episode per week, these serials are not really continuous. In addition, their higher production budgets allow the use of film camera instead of the electronic video camera employed the production of daytime serials. According to them, "prime-time serials and series are combinations of film and broadcasting, with some kinds of programs more like soaps than other".[50] Nevertheless, also Cantor and Pingree see a close relation between daytime - and prime-time serials. That has caused the majority of researchers to define the evening serials as specific variations of an overall soap opera genre.

2.4.   The Soap Opera Form in Britain

In Britain the first radio soap opera only emerged after the firm Reithian principles had been undermined in the course of World War II and its immediate aftermath. Yet, there had been a British radio soap opera during the War *The Front Line Family*, which, however, was not intended for British listeners but was to be broadcast via the BBC World Service to the US and Canada. "(...) the British were keen to tell the world how well they were 'taking it' - and persuade the Americans to join in the fight against Hitler."[51]

In 1948 the serial *Mrs. Dale's Diary* (until 1969)[52] and in 1950 *The Archers* became Britain's first radio soap operas for the 'home front'.

The BBC producers were eager to stress that, for instance, *Mrs. Dale's Diary* was "not a soap opera of the kind which abounds on American day-time radio and is therefore not subject to the restricted rules and practices of sponsors and their agents."[53]

The fact that BBC radio is not subject to commercial sponsorship, has affected that radio serials in Britain, unlike those in the United States, survived despite the decline of the radio audience.

The Archers[54] which started in 1950 has been on the air five days a week ever since.

---

[49] Muriel G. Cantor and Suzanne Pingree, *The Soap Opera* (Beverly Hills, London, New Delhi, 1983) p. 25.

[50] ibid., p. 50.

[51] Peter Buckman, 1984, op.cit., p. 18.

[52] "It concentrated on the everyday lives of the heroine's family, relayed through the story which she told.(...) Mrs. Dale was wife, mother, mother-in-law, grandmother, friend, neighbour, employer, and she juggled her life playing every role. She was unashamedly middle class, but her role as doctor's wife enabled her to cut across class - at least within the programme. (...) listeners were allowed to eavesdrop as Mrs. Dale's thoughts were transferred to the pages of the airwaves." cf. Dorothy Hobson, *Crossroads.*, pp. 28-29.

[53] cf. Peter Buckman (1984, op.cit., p.28) quoting from the editorial of *Mrs. Dale's Diary*.

[54] "The Archers works on the basis of a family story, but one which is much more located in the

In 1987 BBC radio even started a new soap opera *Citizens*. In contrast to *The Archers* which is set in the rural Worcestershire, *Citizens* is set in London and features urban life and its problems.

When *The Archers* started in 1950, the British population still suffered under the post-war food shortage. That is why in those days there existed a close link between *The Archers* editorial office and the Ministry of Agriculture, which saw the serial as an effective vehicle to bring over the latest agricultural findings to the farmers. Even without such an official commission from the ministry, the serial occasionally carries such information. Meanwhile three generations of farmers have progressed from traditional farming to modern intensive farming and back to organic farming.

As shortly before on America television, the form of the continuous serial also became established on British television around the year 1960. As Dorothy Hobson suggests, it was a natural form for the newly established commercial television.

In 1957 Independent Television (ITV) started to broadcast the twice weekly hospital serial *Emergency Ward Ten* (until 1966) and in late 1960 *Coronation Street* appeared in the ITV programme and has remained there ever since.

Coronation Street in a number of aspects constituted an innovation in the soap opera genre. Unlike its American predecessors, it was set in an urban environment and a working-class milieu and drew on the local accent and habits of a real city. Furthermore, it carried, especially in the first two years contemporary social themes.

One of its early producers, Derek Granger, said:

> "(...) and we try to make it as socially telling as possible. It's not respectful of authority. People in the Street make unkind cracks about the Government, the Cabinet, Bomb tests (...)"[55]

In addition to the political connotation, which later decreased, the serial has up to the present distinguished itself from the more melodramatic American soap operas by its comical elements.

As will be explained in more detail in the next chapter, there were three main factors which enabled the private ITV production company Granada (chaired by the Socialist Bernstein family) to produce a popular soap opera in a Social Realist format.

The first factor seemed to be the Socialist leanings of the Bernstein family and their patronage over the North of England.

The second factor was constituted by the Social Realist tendency in the theatre, literature and film which had emerged in the late fifties and was the dominant

---

fictional village of Ambridge, and the sense of locality and farming within the country community has always been a strong theme within the programme." cf. Dorothy Hobson, *Crossroads...*, p. 27.

[55] W.J. Weatherby, "Granada's Camino Real", *Contrast* (Summer 1962), p. 85.

cultural trend at the time of the serials' inception.

The third factor is related to the so-called 'affluence debate' at that particular time and individual contributions to the debate, such as Richard Hoggart's book *The Uses of Literacy* (1957).

Coronation Street coined the type of the Social Realist soap opera, which other serials in Britain and elsewhere followed.

In Britain it is mainly the Channel Four serial *Brookside*[56] (since 1982) and the BBC1 production *EastEnders* (since 1985) which represent that type of the continuous long-running serial.

Especially, *EastEnders* which is set in a lower-class milieu in the East End of London has a lot in common with *Coronation Street*. The BBC audience survey cited before, which was conducted before production, revealed how much viewers' predispositions concerning a possible new BBC soap were influenced by *Coronation Street*. One result of the survey was that

"(...) Manchester turned out to be the most popular location overall, but London was a good second choice with Birmingham a poor third. The survey results clearly showed that a working-class neighbourhood was much more appealing than either a middle class or a mixed class neighbourhood."[57]

But both, *EastEnders* and *Brookside*, have been more explicitly committed than *Coronation Street* in recent years to tackling contemporary social issues such as homosexuality, racism, rape, drug addiction etc.

Coronation Street on the other hand has been given credit for its humour and its less explicit educational tone.

Apart from these three long-term continuous serials there are two other soap operas which for a long time have been part of the regular British television programme. These are *Emmerdale Farm* which has been broadcast on ITV since 1972 and *Crossroads* which was shown on ITV between 1964 and 1988. *Emmerdale Farm* which is set in a Yorkshire village is often seen as a television equivalent of *The Archers*.

Crossroad[58] which was set in a motel near Birmingham sometimes included topics of social concern such as the problems of alcoholism, a mentally handicapped boy and black people. Nevertheless, it always existed in the shadow of *Coronation Street* with critics regularly denouncing it as 'badly written' and 'badly acted'.[59]

Coronation Street does not only constitute the prototype of the Social Realist

---

[56] *Brookside* is set in a private housing estate in Liverpool.

[57] Vivien Marles and Nadine Nohr, op.cit., p. 69.

[58] For further information on *Crossroads* cf. Dorothy Hobson, *Crossroads: The Drama of A Soap Opera*.

[59] cf. for instance Christopher Dunkley, "Brand New Programmes Kick off The Year". *Financial Times* 16. 1. 1988.

Rita Fairclough a long-standing (since the mid-70s) CS-character with young Jenny Bradley, the daughter of Rita's 'murderous' ex-lover Alan Bradley

The young CS-couple Steph and Des Barnes

Brookside

The British director Ron Jones and his team while recording a *Lindenstraße* scene

The Sarikakis, the owners of the Greek restaurant in *Lindenstraße* and Elisabeth Dressler, Vasily's German mother in law   Photo: D. Krüger, WDR

The malicious caretaker's wife Else Kling
Photo: D. Krüger, WDR

soap opera. As it still continues, it also exists in a competitive interrelation with the other soap operas shown on British television. Especially the competition with the more modern, aggresive and socially outspoken *EastEnders* entailed a number of changes in the programme.

Comparable to several of the American daytime serials in the seventies, *Coronation Street* at the end of the eighties was given a 'face-lift', which included modernisation of some of the *Streets* interior settings and the introduction of a range of new younger characters, some from racial minorities.

It also competed with the customary elements of crime in *EastEnders*, such as the late 1988 storylines involving an East-End gang and Den, the shifty publican of the serial who committed arson and for months was depicted as a prisoner until he was finally found dead. In early 1989 *Coronation Street* retalliated by also including violent crime, which included the stabbing to death of long-standing character Brian Tilsley and the attempted murder of Rita Fairclough by Alan Bradley, the man she lived with.

But unlike *EastEnders* at that stage, *Coronation Street* then was also given more colour and a moderate quantity of glamour, above all reflected in the now more affluently dressed and furnished characters. The latter is perhaps a silent concession made in the competition with the more glamorous soap operas from the US and Australia.[60] But it may also be a reflection of the spirit of aspiration brought about by the economic age of Thatcher, which subsequently also affected *EastEnders*.

In addition, the serial started to be shown three times - instead of only two times a week and like *EastEnders* and *Brookside*, it is now repeated as omnibus-edition at the week-end. Those changes had the desired effect that by the year 1988/89 *Coronation Street* was back to being Britain's most popular soap opera.

2.5.   Coronation Street As Model For The First German Soap Opera

In 1988 Alessandro Silj and others investigated the television serials/series of five West European countries (Ireland, Italy, Great Britain, France and West Germany).

One result of the study was that the only countries in which the long-running continuous serial had a long tradition were Britain and Ireland and to a certain extent France. In the other countries investigated other types of serials/series predominated prior to the import of the two American prime time soap operas *Dallas*

---

[60] *Dallas* and *Dynasty* were also popular in Britain, though there were always thought to be very different from the indigenous serials. Besides in 1988 the Australian soap opera *Neighbours* became extremely popular, in particular with young viewers. This was very surprising, since until then Australian soap operas were always termed as 'badly writen' and 'badly acted' and just good enough to be shown during low-audience time slots.

and *Dynasty* in the early eighties.[61]

In West Germany the most frequently used formats were series of about 13 self-contained episodes or mini-series of three to six episodes. However, some very popular family series in the fifties and sixties such as *Die Schölermanns* and *Die Firma Hesselbach* kept on reappearing in new sets, so that the total number of episodes could amount to well over a hundred.[62] But Silj et al. found out that West German television, like French television, reacted to the enormous success of *Dallas* (which was first shown in 1981) and *Dynasty* (first shown in 1983) by producing indigenous long-term serials. In late 1985, the second channel ZDF started to broadcast *Schwarzwaldklinik* (Black Forest Clinic) and the first channel ARD offered *Lindenstraße* (Linden Street) to its viewers.

ZDF's *Schwarzwaldklinik* was broadcast once a week in blocks of 24 episodes of 45 minutes length. Unlike, *Lindenstraße* or the French serial *Chateauvallon*, *Schwarzwaldklinik* did not consist of narratively open episodes but of self-contained episodes, though the central setting of a residential clinic remained the same and a number of loose overall storylines were employed. It is therefore questionable from a narrative point of view whether *Schwarzwaldklinik* can be called a soap opera, though in Germany it is sometimes referred to as one. Stylistically, it synthesizes elements which are popular with German audiences: elements from the *Heimatfilm* with its glorification of landscapes and folk life, elements from the *Arztfilm* (stories about doctors and hospitals with their images of trustworthy, authoritarian doctors, stylistically different from such serials as *General Hospital* and *Emergency Ward Ten* and elements from the typical German family series of the 1960s. Thanks to those ingredients, Schwarzwaldklinik achieved a popularity (audience shares of 60 % and more) which is unparalleled by both *Lindenstraße* and the imported American serials. Yet, the series was not meant to last indefinitely and thus was terminated in spring 1989, after 70 episodes.
Subsequently, ZDF produced two serials, *Das Erbe der Guldenburgs* (The Heritage of The Guldenburgs) and *Rivalen der Rennbahn* (Rivals of The Race Course), for the same Saturday evening time slot, which had a more continuous narrative structure and resembled, like the French serial *Chateauvallon* the American evening serials in setting and content.

In contrast to the newly developed ZDF serial formats, ARD with *Lindenstraße* introduced a home-produced continuous serial, which is modelled on the British Social Realist type of soap opera, but which is also marked by some in-

---

[61] Alessandro Silj et al., *East of Dallas: The European Challenge to American Television*, (London, 1988).

[62] Jan-Uwe Rogge, Tagträume oder warum Familienserien so beliebt sind. Zur Geschichte, Machart und psycho-sozialen Funktion von Familienserien im deutschen Fernsehen. In: *Medienpolitik* edited by Landeszentrale für politische Bildung Baden-Würtemberg (Stuttgart, 1987).

gredients from the more melodramatic American serials. Those elements are implanted into the quite authentic German milieu of a residential community in a Munich street. The serial which is shown once a week for half an hour has open episodes and was right from the start designed to last for more than 200 episodes and although it does not achieve audience figures (mostly ratings of around 30 %) which are as stunningly high as those of *Schwarzwaldklinik* at its time, it is likely to last for much longer.

Lindenstraße was the first serial in the Federal Republic that is subject to the tight and streamlined production schedule of a continuous programme. Due to organisational reasons within the first public channel, only one episode per week is produced and episodes are normally completed ten weeks in advance. So far two British directors have on and off worked on the serial, sharing their greater experience in continuous serial production.

The central setting of *Lindenstraße* is a block of flats in a Munich street and some adjacent buildings, such as a Greek restaurant, a doctor's surgery, a café, a hairdresser's salon, a flower shop and an Italian snack bar.
Unlike *Coronation Street* and *EastEnders* but similar to *Brookside*, the serial does not represent a specific social milieu. Rather, the locality of *Lindenstraße* with its cross-section of characters whose social identities range from lower middle class to professional middle class and business class, seems to aim at a representation of what is generally understood as an 'average urban neighbourhood in Germany'. Largely consistent with that concept, *Lindenstraße* has always included a range of characters from different national backgrounds (the owners of the Greek restaurant, a Vietnamese refugee, a French young woman, an Italian Jew, an adopted child from Mexico and immigrants from Poland of German stock). In addition, the serial's representation of minority groups is completed by two regular homosexual characters and recently a handicapped teenager.

Apart from the basic idea and a certain set of narrative conventions, it seems to have adopted from *Coronation Street* and other British serials also the formulae for some of the characters. A most obvious example is the character of Else Kling that in some respects is modelled on the late Ena Sharples who appeared in *Coronation Street* for eighteen years (1960 to 1978). But in a number of aspects Else Kling also deviates from the Ena Sharples character type.
Ena Sharples, already in her sixties when *Coronation Street* started, used to be the caretaker of the street's chapel the Glad Tidings Mission. Else Kling at a similar age is a bossy caretaker's wife who supports or rather dominates her husband in his work for the residential community in *Lindenstraße*. Like another long-standing *Coronation Street* character, Hilda Ogden, she also works as cleaner, which increases her opportunities to spot other people's secrets and to swiftly disseminate them in the community.
Else Kling like Ena Sharples is waspish with a vicious streak, strong-headed, adhering to a set of conservative principles and most of the time scowling.
But while brusque and hard-edged Ena Sharples was always ready to charge into

battle at the first sign of pomposity and authority and "kindness itself to people in trouble"[63], Else Kling is prone to behave in a creeping and servile manner in the presence of anybody with the slightest sign of authority and more likely to shun people in trouble. While both Ena Sharples and Hilda Ogden, despite their obvious lack of formal education, displayed a quick common-sense wit, Else Kling is simply stupid and reactionary.

Ena Sharples and Hilda Ogden were recognizable as carricatures contributing to the comedy of *Coronation Street*. But Else Kling at the beginning of *Lindenstraße* was one-dimensionally mean and malicious. Only when audience surveys revealed that the character did not appeal to many viewers, she was given some softer features. But the latter are mainly constituted by a certain eruptive, melodramatic emotionality, which seems not to increase the vigour of the character.

In some ways the character of Else Kling is symptomatic of some deficit in original and strong character and a lack of comedy in *Lindenstraße*. Apart from occasional show-biz interludes performed by some of the regular characters and some quaint little incidents, the serial mostly exhausts itself in Realism which, as is common in soap opera, easily diverges into Melodrama. The latter tendency is enhanced by the fact that in the German serial, like in American soap operas but unlike *in Coronation Street* and other British serials, off-screen music is employed as a dramaturgical device.

However, on rare occasions the serial makers have taken recourse to Brechtian alienation technics to subvert Realism and Melodrama.

Partly due to the less strenuous production schedule in comparison with British serials, there is more emphasis on visualisation in the German serial, which is, for example, reflected in the more detailed portrayal of backgrounds.

Lindenstraße like the British serials, contains references to contemporary events, as for example, national elections, the disaster of Chernobyl, the Gulf war etc. and social issues such as homosexuality, AIDS and racism. Especially, with the recent Gulf war and the crisis in Lithuania the serial has made an extra effort to be topical in those references. The sound track of some scenes which were singled out for that purpose beforehand, were altered up to three days before showing.

Since problems of the environment and fear of right-wing political tendencies preoccupy a larger fraction of German - than of British society, *Lindenstraße* more than its British counterparts is devoted to the treatment of such issues.

---

[63] cf. Hilary Kingsley's characterisation of Ena Sharples in: H. Kingsley, *Soap Box: The Papermac Guide to Soap Opera*, (London, 1988), pp. 127 - 128.

3. THE STRUCTURE OF INDEPENDENT TELEVISION AND THE PRODUCTION CONTEXT OF CORONATION STREET

3.1. The Changing Structure of Independent Television

Since 1955 when commercial television was first introduced to supplement the public service broadcasting system of the BBC (British Broadcasting Corporation), broadcasting in Britain has been organized as 'duopole'.

That implies that the BBC is almost exclusively financed by viewers' licence fees, whereas the private network solely relies on advertising revenue.

Prior to the advent of celestial television, the terrestrial television duopole in Britain had gradually come to embrace four channels: BBC1, BBC2 (since 1964), the first commercial channel ITV (Independent Television) and since 1982 an additional commercial service Channel Four.

Currently, the British broadcasting system is, however, undergoing massive changes. These were initially brought about through the new transmission technologies of cable and satellite, which allowed for an indefinite number of channels. The expansion of the technical possibilities of broadcasting required new legal and political foundations. The provisions made by the Conservative government under Margret Thatcher culminated in the highly controversial 1990 Broadcasting Act. The new legislation affects a rigorous deregulation of the traditional commercial sector, while the BBC (which is not governed by parliamentary legislation but by a Royal Charter due for renewal in 1996) is at the present stage left largely untouched but is likely to be affected in a second phase.

The 1954 Television Act, which constituted the first legal basis of commercial television in Britain, provided a federal structure for the then newly established ITV system. Up to now that federal structure has embraced 15 private production companies who have held licences for 14 regional franchise areas (London being serviced by two companies), into which Britain is subdivided. Franchise holders are first of all required to produce or procure programmes for their respective region. In addition, they are obliged to contribute material to the joint ITV network programme, relative to their size and capacity.

After the coming into force of the new Broadcasting Act on 1 January 1991, a radical relocation of franchises could take place. For, the Act prescribes that franchises are to be auctioned to the highest bidder provided he/she fullfills a number of requirements concerning the range and standard of programmes.

The previous legislation which governed ITV until the end of 1990 laid down that the private production companies were to be controlled by a public body, the Independent Television Authority, which in 1973 became the Independent Broadcasting Authority (IBA) (taking over additional control over a then newly established network of commercial radio stations).

Until the end of 1990 the IBA was responsible for issuing, renewing and (in rare cases) withdrawing the broadcasting licences. Another task of the Authority was to guarantee that the three traditional principles of public broadcasting in Britain: taste, decency and impartiality were also followed by the commercial broadcasters. Furthermore, the IBA had to ensure balance in the proportion of information, education and entertainment, in the ratio of national versus regional broadcasts and in the percentage of foreign versus British productions. The Authority also had to observe compliance with the rules of the code of advertising.

Part of that control was exerted through IBA employees' chairing the Programme Controllers Group, the task of whom was to survey the programme schedules which had to be submitted by the programme suppliers before broadcasting.

A further responsibility of the IBA was to provide the staff and technical facilities for the transmission of the commercial programmes..

In return the 15 production companies had to pay rental money to the IBA and since 1964 a direct tax on their advertising revenues, the levy.

Under the new Broadcasting Act the IBA and the Cable Authority which since 1985 had warranted a 'light touch' regulation of British satellite and cable services, were abolished.

Instead, the law provides that the control over terrestrial and non-terrestrial commercial television which the two bodies previously administered seperately with different intensity, is to be transferred to a new institution, the Independent Television Commission (ITC). Whereas responsibility over terrestrial and non-terrestrial commercial radio is handed over to the newly established Radio Authority (RA).

Both new controlling bodies are designed to adopt rather the more relaxed code of control of the previous Cable Authority than that of the IBA.

Nevertheless, the ITC's touch upon the terrestrial channels is meant to be heavier than that on domestic satellite channels. Thus, licences for domestic satellite channels are to be issued by the ITC for 15 years, while the terrestrial licences expire after only 10 years.[1]

While there are only a minimum of rules regulating the range and quality of programmes on domestic satellite services, licence holders for channel 3 (replacing the previous ITV channel), channel 4 and the new channel 5 (in planning) have to comply with more clearly defined prerequirements and programme standards. In theory those are quite far reaching, except that the control system granted to the ITC is not as tight as the one which was previously allowed to the IBA.

Thus, the law imparts substantial authority to the ITC in the licensing process to examine applicants for Channel 3 and Channel 5 licences.

The ITC is also given the power to impose fines and withdraw licences in the case of later deviations from the legal requirements on licence holders. But the judgement of the ITC is clearly limited by the legal provision that a licence has to be

---

[1] cf. Broadcasting Act 1990 published by Her Majesty's Stationary Office.

granted to the highest bidder provided he/she can prove the capability of sup-plying the range and quality of programmes prescribed.

Once licences have been issued, the ITC may monitor the programmes provided by the licensees to keep control and measure them against a code of standards. But the law does not allow in advance control of programme schedules any more.[2] Likewise, the ITC does no longer own and control the technical transmission equipment of commercial television.

Due to differences in the size of franchise areas (and consequently in the advertising revenues) and to previous concentration processes, the ITV system has never been a federation of equals. Rather, it has for a long time been dominated by the 'Big Five', the five largest companies: Thames TV, Tyne Tees, Associated Television, Yorkshire Television and Granada Television which have held the lic-ences for the most densely populated areas in Britain (London, the Midlands and the metropolitan areas of the north).

The 'Big Five' have also been called 'network companies', for they contributed by far the majority of the material to the ITV national programme and also supple-mented the regional broadcasts of the smaller companies.

While the 1990 Broadcasting Act provides that Channel 3 will retain a regional structure (nine large and six small francises), concentration processes are likely to be enhanced through a number of factors. One such factor is the in-creased competition for advertising money. This is brought about through the establishment of the new Channel 5, the licensees of which have not to fulfill any requirements concerning regional programming, and through a renewed Channel Four, which henceforth has to sell its advertising time independently of the reg-ional ITV companies.

Besides, growing competition and increased economic pressure are likely to im-pede programme exchanges at favourable prices within the Channel 3 network, from which in the past especially the smaller regional companies benefitted

The law already foreshadows concentration by allowing parallel ownership of one large and one small Channel 3 franchise if they are not adjacent to each-other. Under certain circumstances it is also possible that licensees can have their licence 'temporarily' extended to supply services in another franchise area. Besides, the law allows a restricted cross-ownership in different terrestrial and sat-ellite channels.

In the past ITV companies have also contributed a substantial part to the programme of Channel Four. The purpose of Channel Four was, and under the new legislation remains, to supplement the majority- oriented ITV (channel 3) programme (comparable to BBC2 supplementing BBC1) by providing more in-tellectual and innovative programmes and by catering for minority tastes and in-terests. In aid of these objectives, it has been an important characteristic of Chan-

---

[2] cf. Broadcasting Act 1990, Section 11, 3.

nel Four that it obtained a large proportion of its programmes from independent production companies[3].

The main task of Channel Four (also under the new legislation) is to procure - rather than to produce programmes. In 1993 it will, however, lose its present organisational form as a trust and will instead be transformed into a corporation. The Channel Four Corporation will receive its broadcasting licence from the ITC. Similar to the 15 ITV companies, Channel Four was until the end of 1990 subject to the control of the IBA. But, unlike the regional ITV companies, Channel Four so far has only been indirectly dependent on advertising money. Instead, its finance relied on a levy which the IBA took from the ITV companies. The latter could in return draw revenue from selling the Channel Four advertising time in their franchise areas.

By virtue of the new legislation, this system of financing Channel Four is to be changed. Besides, the prescribed minimum share of independent productions will be decreased to 25 %, corresponding with the share laid down for all the other private channels and which the *Peacock Report*[4] recommended for the BBC.
As has already been indicated, the finance of the Channel Four Corporation and programme will in future mainly rely on direct advertising revenue, though with one modification.
That modification is due to the fact that the public service element in Channel Four is much more emphasized than with the other commercial channels under the new legislation.[5] To provide a financial safeguard for that element, Channel Four has a guaranteed minimum income of 14 % of the total revenue of all terrestrial commercial channels (this includes mainly Channel 3 and Channel 5). If in any one year the Channel Four Corporation falls short of obtaining that minimum, the ITC is entitled to raise the difference by imposing a levy on the Channel 3 licence holders, which, however, is not allowed to exceed 2 % of the total qualifiying revenue.[6]

3.2. The Production Company Granada

The role of the Granada television production company in the new era of commercial broadcasting in Britain has yet to be defined[7]. But as one of the 'Big

---

[3] These are production companies which are neither permanently attached to the ITV system nor to the BBC.

[4] *The Peacock Report On The Financing of The BBC* was published in 1986.

[5] In Section 25, (2a) of the 1990 Broadcasting Act it says "Channel 4 is provided as a public service for disseminating information, education and entertainment". Furthermore, the law requires "a high general standard in all respects".

[6] cf. Section 26 (2a and 4) of the 1990 Broadcasting Act.

[7] The final decision on the Channel 3 franchises are taken between September and December 1991.

Five' franchise holders in the still existing ITV network and with shares in several British Satellite services, the film industry, American television companies and established links with television companies in Canada and major EEC countries it does have a strong position. According to official statements[8], Granada is confident to regain the franchise. In addition, it has expressed interest in taking over one of two smaller franchises.

Granada Television Network Ltd. is a subsidiary of the Granada Group Ltd., a highly diversified vertical conglomerate.[9]
Apart from television production, the Granada Group is also involved in television set rental, property investment and development, insurance, bingo social clubs, cinemas, motorway services and book publishing.[10]

Granada television began transmission in Lancashire and Yorkshire in 1956. The first licence awarded to the company allowed only the provision of programmes for weekdays while the weekend programmes in the North were provided by another company. The 1968 licence enabled Granada to also provide weekend programmes but excluded the Yorkshire area from the franchise. 'Granadaland', as the franchise had been dubbed, was henceforth situated in the North-West of England stretching from North Wales, across the Pennines and north to the Lake District with Liverpool and Manchester as major centres.

The headquarter of Granada television is the TV Centre in Manchester, which held the first studio in Britain specially built for television. But Granada also has bases in other major cities of the franchise area, especially Liverpool where in 1986 one of the most advanced electronic news centres in Europe was built.

A majority shareholder in Granada Ltd. were and continue to be the Bernstein family. The two brothers Sidney and Cecil Bernstein were the first managing directors of Granada TV Network Ltd.
In 1979 Sidney handed over the chairmanship of the Granada Group to Cecil's son Alexander who still holds that position. Alexander Bernstein then became also deputy managing director of Granada television. Whereas now he is no longer officially involved in Granada television. After Cecil Bernstein's death in 1983 and his brother Sydney's later illness, the direct influence of the London-based Bernstein family on Granada television has decreased.

The Jewish Bernstein family are said to have traditionally supported the Labour Party, which cast them as Socialist millionaires. Sidney Bernstein was in-

---

[8] According to a statement by Granada press officer Helen Webb on 4 March 1991.

[9] The Granada Group is much more diversified than the Groups which own the other ITV franchises.

[10] cf. Richard Paterson, The Production Context of *Coronation Street*. In: Richard Dyer et al., op. cit., pp. 53-54.

itially a strong opponent of commercial television, the introduction of which in the fifties was mainly lobbied by a strong industrial interest group[11].

Despite that critical attitude, he is said to have been the first to apply for a licence after the Conservative majority in Parliament had decided in favour of commercial television.

Before Granada television started transmission in 1956, the main areas of business in which the Granada Group was involved, were the operation of a chain of cinemas and theatres and a number of retail shops.

Sidney Bernstein's philosophy is often summed up by the following statement:

> "'It's wrong for a Socialist to feel ashamed of making a success of our type of business'. And again, while the capitalist system lasts, 'I don't see why we should let the big boys have it all'."[12]

As managing director of Granada television Sidney Bernstein is remembered by employees as a paternalistic and often autocratic personality - some refer to him as a 'benevolent despot'.[13]

Part of Sidney Bernstein's and Granada's benevolent despotism has been expressed in an outspoken attachment to the region, reflected in an innovative range of regional programmes but also in the sponsorship of festivals, exhibitions and cultural and economic institutions. Granada has invariably professed the aim to strengthen the identity of the region and diminish domination from London. That is why great concern is taken to keep up the image that "the interests and outlook of the great majority of people working in it, including members of the Board, are North-Western and not metropolitan."[14]

Despite their Socialist leanings, it without doubt was not the home-grown culture of the northern franchise area which made the founders of Granada select it as base for their later broadcasting imperium. Instead, it were the following economic facts that counted:

> "Ninety-two per cent of the population live in urban areas, the region is ideal for test marketing; it can reasonably be served with a single news service; it has the four best football teams in the country; and it rains more on the west than on the east side of the Pennines, which perhaps explains why relatively more Granadaland viewers watch television (...)"[15]

---

[11] cf. Harold Wilson, *Pressure Group: The Campaign for Commercial Television in England*, (New Brunswick, 1961).

[12] "The Man Who Became Infamous", *New Statesman* (14 February 1959) in: E. Buscombe (ed.), op. cit., p. 65.

[13] cf. John Wyver, "An Outline Sketch", in E. Buscombe (ed.), p. 3.

[14] Extract from an official company statement of policy, in: E. Buscombe (ed.), op. cit.

[15] John Wyver, "An Outline Sketch". In: E. Buscombe (ed.), op. cit., p. 11.

In order to attract and satisfy advertisers who are Granada television's major source of income, the company today offers a substantial range of services, which include not only the facilities for making commercials plus the appropriate advise, but also research facilities and a Retail Sales Force which can be used to effectively sell a product into the independent trade after an advertising campaign.

Yet, despite its profit-oriented character, Granada has acquired a reputation for combining entertainment with social responsibility in its programme.
Already in 1962, during the investigations for the *Pilkington Report*[16], Richard Hoggart the author of *The Uses of Literacy*, who sat on the Pilkington Committee, singled out "(...) the area of good ITV things such as Coronation Street (...)" and other Granada productions.
Although Hoggart and the majority of the Commitee critized the then young commercial television for sacrificing programme standards for the maximization of advertising profits, Hoggart conceded, "there you seem to have a man who is interested in television itself. Bernstein puts into it things which are expressions of his own excitement".[17]

Over the years Granada has increased its credits for radicalism, innovation and quality, especially in the production of documentary and current affairs programmes but also in the making of television drama.
If it failed to regain its present franchise, it would be left with the option of continuing in the television business as an independent production company.

3.3.   The More Immediate Production Context of Coronation Street

The production of *Coronation Street* in the studios of the Granada Television Centre in Manchester, like the production of any continuous serial, relies on a tight time-schedule and a high degree of work division within the production team. This has been the case virtually from the beginning of the serial but has been enhanced since autumn 1989 with the production of three weekly episodes.

Even Tony Warren who still appears in the credit title as originator of the serial only wrote the scripts of the first five episodes entirely himself. When those had been accepted by Granada, H.V. Kershaw joined Warren in writing the scripts for the next seven episodes to complete the initial 'trial' set of twelve episodes.

---

[16] *The Pilkington Report*, published in 1962, mainly investigated the achievements of the BBC and the newly established ITV and made suggestions for a second public channel (BBC2). Within the British broadcasting system it has become customary to appoint such committees when major decisions for the future of broadcasting have to be taken. More recent reports are the *Annan Report* (1977), the *Hunt Report* (1982) and the already cited *Peacock Report* (1986).

[17] Richard Hoggart, "TV in a Free Society". *Contrast*, 2 (1962-63), p. 10.

The acceptance of Warren's project by Granada is to a large extent credited to Harry Elton, a Canadian expert in commercial television, and at that time Granada's Executive Producer of Drama. It is likely that Elton's transatlantic experience made him sense Warren's serial idea as a likely formula of success.

Part of the process, during which the serial became institutionalized in the Granada Television Centre, was the establishment of a 'Coronation Street office'. Although the producer was in the past formally responsible to the Head of Drama, the 'Coronation Street office' has become increasingly autonomous. Due to restructuration processes within Granada, the 'Coronation Street Office' was in 1988 transferred from the Department of Drama to the newly established Department of Entertainment[18] without major alterations in its status.

The office is serviced by a producer, a script editor, a programme planner, a programme historian, four storyline writers, a public relations officer and secretarial staff. Attached to the office are a number of itinerant directors with their production assistants and technical staff, a group of approximately 12 freelance writers and about thirty regular actors. *Coronation Street* today also has its own studio facilities which are not shared by other production teams.

For a long time "the Street was built in the studio and the cobblestones were painted on the studio floor."[19] Only after electronic editing had facilitated the production of episodes in parts which could be joined together in the editing suite, a Street set outside the studio was built. It is situated right near the Granada TV Centre in Manchester and consists of only facades and the back walls.

Key positions in the production of *Coronation Street* and other continuous serials are that of the producer who bears overall responsibility and that of the storyline editor who is responsible for the content of the scripts and who also determines the long-term development of storylines. Whereas the directors' position is less influencial, mainly due to the highly conventionalized style of shooting. Directors normally only stay with the show for a limited time and then move on to other productions.

Mervyn Watson worked as producer of the serial from 1983 to 1985 and took over again at the beginning of 1989 to carry out the changes in the serial. He said that the production of three weekly episodes required a 50 % increase in backroom - and technical staff. Whereas only two or three additional actors joined the regular team.[20]

The serial also prides itself on having been a 'training camp', or at least a secure source of income, for a number of producers, directors and writers, who later had outstanding careers inside or outside television. Some examples are playwright

---

[18] The Department of Entertainment is the 'editorial roof' of *Coronation Street* and two other continuous serials and several situation comedies and quiz shows.

[19] H.V. Kershaw, op. cit., p. 179.

[20] Mervyn Watson said this on 21 February 1991 in a telephone interview conducted by the author.

Jack Rosenthal, Jim Allen and Peter Eckersley who regarded script-witing for *Coronation Street* "as useful training in producing economical and pointed dialogue to a tight deadline."[21]

The production routine of the serial has for a long time been based on a three-week rota.

Each three-week production period is started by a production conference:

> "Every third Monday the producer meets with his writers, his storyline writers and the casting director to plan the stories for a further six episodes. Plans are laid some ten weeks in advance which is to say that a story conference held at the beginning of January would be discussing episodes which would be seen on the screen from mid March to early April."[22]

Since 1989 the number of episodes planned on the three-weekly meetings has increased from six to nine. Those episodes are part of a broader framework which is mapped out on long-term conferences held periodically.

Barry Hill who is a regular writer for *Coronation Street* but who in 1988 also worked as a 'stand-in storyline writer' describes the latter's job as follows:

> "Where to start? First, a summary of the story points to be included, as agreed at a conference of all the writers ten days previously. Then the task of working out the cast list for the two episodes - who do we really need? Who can't we have because of holiday commitments? From whom can we get best value in peripheral incidents? (...)
> What use could we make of LMVR? Would we get more value out of Brian Tilsley's garage. Perhaps we would get more use out of Alf Roberts' shop?"[23]

After the episodes for one three-week period have been outlined by the four storyline writers, each episode is allocated to a different script-writer. Sometimes two consecutive episodes in which something dramatic happens are written by one and the same writer. With the new production output there are now about 12 regular writers working on the team who may be supplemented by occasional writers. When the writers have finished their 26-minutes scripts, these have to pass the script editor before they are handed over to the directors. Despite the collective nature of the script, it is the script-writer who in the credit title at the end of an episode is referred to as the author.

The recording of the serial is geared to a four-week turn-round. For, there are at any one time four directors working on the serial. This implies that director

---

[21] Peter Buckman, op. cit., p. 96.

[22] H.V. Kershaw, *The Street where I Live*, ((Granada) London, 1981).

[23] This quote is taken from a diary describing his day in television on 1 November 1988, which was completed by Barry Hill in the 'One Day in The Life of Television' project commissioned by the British Film Institute.

one is in his first week of preperation, director two is in his second week of preperation, while director three is in his actual production week and director four is in his post-production week, during which the material is edited.

Watson inferred that, unlike other serials, the three episodes of one week are still shot chronologically by the same director in one week, instead of chopping the episodes up in such a way that, for instance, all outside scenes or all the scenes set in one particular studio set are shot together. "We would lose control otherwise" said Watson.

According to Mervyn Watson, schooting and recording takes place on six days from Sunday to Friday, with Saturday as a free day which may, however, be turned into a working day if something on the previous days went wrong.
At the time when only two weekly episodes were broadcast the production work could be restricted to five days a week. According to Mervyn Watson, the one day increase in production time is in no way relative to the increase in the material produced. Yet he thinks that the production standards of the serial have not suffered, though he thinks it unlikely that the team could go beyond that.[24]

According to Watson's description, the weekly time schedule starts with Sunday for the shooting of location scenes in the city. Afterall one of the changes in the programme was "to geographically expand the world of the inhabitants of the Street"[25].
On Monday the outside scenes in the studio precinct are rehearsed and shot. Tuesday is reserved for block rehearsals[26]. Wednesday is for rehearsals of the inside scenes (the majority of scenes). Whereas the final shooting of those scenes occurs on Thursday and Friday.

Sarah Harding who has worked as director on *Coronation Street* on and off, describes the rehearsal day (still prior to the production of a third weekly episode) as follows:

"(...) is my favourite day on The Street. It's the one opportunity for me to work on the acting, interpretation and focus of scenes. Although the schedule is very tight, about 30 scenes to rehearse in 5 1/2 hours, there's a lot you can do in a day and I'm pleased to find the actors still so responsive to direction."[27]

However, like in most continuous serials, it is the actors who know their characters best and who have to work closely with the different directors to inter-

---

[24] He said this in the interview mentioned in Fn. 3.

[25] ibid.

[26] According to Virginia Oakey's *Dictionary of Film and Telvision Terms* this means "to determine the position of camera, crew and cast, and cast movements before shooting a particular scene".

[27] Sarah Harding in her diary for 1 November 1988, which she completed for the BFI project 'One Day in The Life of Television'.

prete the script in line with the 'personality' of the character they impersonate. Sarah Harding refers to an incident during which the actress Sue Jenkins who at that time was acting a *Coronation Street* character (Goria) who had pinched her girl-friend's man. "Sue isn't keen on saying the last line 'Sandra who?' in reply to Pete's 'still worried about Sandra?' after a kiss. She 's worried that it makes Gloria out to be a bitch and unsympathetic."[28] The director and the actress jointly decide that the line is to be played playfully and not maliciously and Sue Jenkins 'finds it works' with her character.

The following example shows that actors also take care on the outward appearance of their particular character. In her description of one day in television, *Coronation Street* actress Barbara Knox (she impersonates newsagent Rita Fairclough) infers: " (...) Wardrobe department up to discuss our costumes for this week's episode. I have had some of my jumpers for donkey's years, it is time a few were thrown, but our budget is tight."[29]

Barbara Knox and Brian Mosley, another *Coronation Street* actor, regret that there is so little time for rehearsals. Mosley, who acts grocer Alf Roberts, particularly dislikes that they are not allowed to rehearse with props before the actual day of recording. The pace of production of the serial may also enhance the anxiety which some actors feel towards the shooting and editing process. Mosley infers: "The anxiety (...), of making scenes work, of relationships with other characters. The sometime frustration of not knowing if interactions between us will be lost for the sake of 'shots'. The underlying uncertainty of the value of some scenes or parts of a scene, and whether all the work will be wasted or cut."[30]

According to producer Mervyn Watson, *Coronation Street* episodes under the new production schedule are recorded only three weeks before they are shown on television. If something unexpected happens, such as a key actor falling ill "we have to quickly rewrite the scripts".

---

[28] ibid.

[29] Sean Day-Lewis, *One Day in The Life of Telvision*, (London, Glasgow, Toronto, Sydney, Auckland, 1989), p. 148.

[30] ibid., p. 149.

4. THE NATURE AND EFFECTS OF REALISM, NOSTALGIA, COMEDY AND CAMP IN CORONATION STREET

4.1. Soap Opera Realism and Social Realism

Peter Buckman stresses that in soap opera - like in any television programme - "reality is an artificial thing that is always being manipulated for the plot's benefit".[1] According to Buckman, the only essential difference between American and British soap operas in terms of realism is that "the Americans employ a heightened reality - character and setting that are larger than life but totally consistent and convincing within their own terms of reference". Whereas the British go for what he calls "a 'flattened reality', a middlebrow, nuts-and-bolts, everyday sort of reality", which on the whole is unglamorous, even mundane (but still absorbing to the viewer).[2]

Robert Allen who, as indicated before, analyses the soap opera as a textual system which has been shaped by social and commercial influences, strongly refutes a simple and immediate relationship between soap opera and reality.

The ways in which reality is reverberated[3] in *Coronation Street* are shaped to a great extent by the serial's cumulative tradition built up over a period of 30 years. In addition, reality is moulded by an amalgamation of various more general sets of conventions. The three more general sets of conventions which people have discerned in the programme are, as suggested before, the conventions of the soap opera genre, the conventions of literary and theatrical Social Realism as it developed during the 1950s and a mixture of comical elements.

What it means to produce a continuous programme which, like *Coronation Street*, embodies a claim to realism but is at the same time highly conventionalized, is reflected in an interview which the then CS producer Susie Hush gave the *Guardian* newspaper in 1974. Despite her initial claim that *Coronation Street* is 'a slice of life'[4] in the North of England, Hush concedes:

---

[1] Peter Buckman, op. cit., p. 45.

[2] Peter Buckman, All..., p. 45.

[3] Fiske and Hartley argue from a semiotic point of view that "(...) reality is never experienced by social man in the raw. Whether the reality in question is the brute force of nature or men's relations with other men, it is always experienced through the mediating structures of language." (cf. Fiske and Hartley, op. cit., p. 161.) The semiotic concept of the role of language can be compared to the role of generic conventions in the television discourse.

[4] The term 'a slice of life' has the connotation of a documentary or at least a realistic or naturalistic fictional representation. According to J.A. Cuddon's *Dictionary of Literary Terms,((Penguin)* Harmondsworth, 1977), p. 635.) it can even be taken as short for a portrait of life "in the raw, factual, visceral and unadulterated by art."

"You can't aim for realism (...) It would be smashing to do a story about squatters, but they would have to be grafted on. You have to work with characters as they've been built up. The programme has a fictional reality which has been established over 14 years"[5]

What Hush describes is a characteristic of the so-called 'Soap Opera Realism'. As has been mentioned elsewhere, other key characteristics of that type of fictional realism are the organisation of the narrated time largely in analogy with the progress of time in real life and the naturalistic depiction of life in a small-scale parochial world with more or less tentative relations to the society as a whole.

Dennis Porter contends that continuous TV serials are very successful in carrying out what he calls "the illusionist ploy of realism".[6] He uses figures of speech to describe the modes of representation in narratives and applies that mind of analysis also to soap opera. According to Porter, any realist narration is metonymic in character. Metonymy, however, is a figure of speech that "purchases vivid compression at the cost of suppression." Porter sees one of the most significant features of soap opera that "it is largely constituted of such suppressions."[7]
Yet, despite the suppressed form of reality which soap opera usually conveys, it is almost invariably associated with a larger reality. Moreover, it is, as Porter infers, conceived as a typical extract of that total reality. This suggests it can have the effect of a synecdoche.

Marion Jordan's analysis of the style of the opening and closing sequences behind the credit titles of *Coronation Street,* seems to suggest that the synecdoche is also an underlying concept of *Coronation Street.* Marion Jordan suggests:

"The title itself sets the programme firmly in a North-country industrial town with its suggestion of nineteenth century terrace houses; and the promise of the small-group world it contains (and the large-scale world of industry and politics it omits) is confirmed by the opening sequence shot over the roofs and the glimpse of 'The Rovers Return' (...) The style of these shots, invariably moving from this long-shot with its suggestion that this is a God's-eye view of the totality of experience, to a mid-shot ground-level view of the street, with its suggestion of the group, to a closer (but not usually close-up) view of some door or interior in Coronation Street, insists on typicality, insists that Coronation Street is a randomly chosen street, one among many; that each house is a randomly chosen house, one among many; and that it can only be in the close examination of textual detail that differences are to be found."[8]

5   R. Thornber, "Why Coronation Street Will Never be The Susie Hush Show", Guardian 13 December 1974, p. 8.

6   Dennis Porter, "Soap Time: Thoughts of a Commodity Art Form" in: Horac Newcomb (ed.), Television: The Critical View. (Oxford, New York, 3rd. ed. 1982), pp. 122-131, p. 125.

7   ibid.

8   Marion Jordan, Realism and Convention. In: Richard Dyer et al., *Television Monograph: Coron-*

In fact, metonymy in *Coronation Street* is not only used as a device in the title but can also be found in many other aspects of the serial. Thus, no more than nine houses in *Coronation Street*, in combination with buildings from some of the adjacent streets, are featured in representation of an entire street or even a whole quarter. Of the actual street and the back-lane behind the houses only stretches are shown from time to time. The use of metonyms is continued in the representation of the interiors of the various houses. There, mainly kitchens and living-rooms are used as settings. Whereas bedrooms or bathrooms, for instance, are rarely depicted.

In a more figurative sense it could be suggested that the programme as a whole is metonymic in at least three ways. First, the programme is metonymic in the sense that the contemporary references which are strewn into the dialogues suggest the small-scale world of *Coronation Street* as a piece of British reality and as part of the overall political - and social structure.

Secondly, a metonymic relationship could be seen to exist between the programme and the region. The programme purports to be about the North, or more particularly about the Manchester area. Yet, in fact the Merseyside area is rarely depicted in the serial, since, as has been said before, location shots are rare for economical reasons (though more frequent in recent years). The main factor therefore which evokes the association with the region is the variety of northern accents with which characters in the serial speak.

Thirdly, the programme is metonymic in its representation of social class. The programme suggests that it is about working-class people in the North of England. What it actually does, however, is to feature a group of people who live in a street of working-class terraced houses, allegedly situated in a quarter that consists entirely of such streets.

In addition, a number of the people who appear in the programme converse in a language that is marked not only by the regional accent but also by slang expressions, which means that characters in *Coronation Street* speak a sociolect that distinguishes them from middle-class people.

Furthermore, it is the strong sense of community in an urban milieu reflected in the programme which, together with the elements mentioned before, constitutes an important aspect of the traditional image of the working class in Britain.

Other aspects which respond to that image are the modest, formerly in some cases even shabby way in which characters are dressed (due to the changes in the overall image of the programme, characters in recent years make a considerably better appearance) and certain traditional working-class attitudes and habits - particularly leisure time activities - such as going to the pub, reading tabloid papers, playing bingo or watching football matches.

However, a look at the occupational structure in *Coronation Street* suggests that the serial was right from the beginning based on a rather unrigorous definition of working class. For, although a number of characters are known to have an

ation Street, (London BFI 1981), pp. 27-39, p. 30.

industrial working-class background, hardly anybody in the programme seems to belong to that section of the working class, which in reality is still the largest group of society.

Traditionally, the majority of characters have always belonged to the upper stratum of the working class or to the lower middle class, with a few characters who can even be classed higher than that.

Thus, Ken Barlow, the aspiring scholarship boy of the early days, has a university degree. Although he has not had the bright and consistent career which seemed to be awaiting him in the early years of the programme, he can still be placed at the fringes of the professional class.

Mike Baldwin, who, despite a lower-class background, as the owner of two factories and shareholder in other enterprises, is an obviously middle-class character. As part of the recent changes in the programme, Baldwin, who also is the employer of some of the women in Coronation Street, is joined in that function by Holdsworth, the manager of a newly opened super-market, who also employs some of the women. Yet, unlike Baldwin, he is not boss and capital owner in one person but rather belongs to the executive class.

Traditionally, many characters in the serial were self-employed, while a still larger number worked as assistants or apprentices of the latter.

Most jobs belong to the service sector, the grittiest being that of a cleaner and a dustman. It is easy to perceive that most of these jobs have the advantage that they do not lead the characters too far away from the *Street*, which would otherwise diminish their value as serial characters. For, in the occupations described above, they can be shown doing their job within the neighbourhood. This would not be possible with an industrial worker, whose place of work would be separated from the home and the community.

A rare example of a character who belonged to the industrial working class proper was Bert Tilsley, a skilled (not even he was an unskilled worker) night-shift worker (so that during the day he could appear in the community) at a local steel-works. He, his wife Ivy and their son Brian moved to the *Street* in 1979.

At the end of 1980 Bert was made redundant because the steel-works closed down. It seems that his place of work was never shown in the programme. For, obviously it would have caused considerable difficulties to define it as an extension of the *Street*, as happens with the other places of work. If Bert Tilsley had been featured performing an exacting routine work in a bustling steel-works, there would have been little opportunity for him to talk, the one activity which is so vital in the soap opera format.

In 1984 Bert Tilsley died of cancer. Until then he seems not to have found another job in heavy industry. His time of long-term unemployment, however, does not appear too problematic since it was eased by the fact that there were opportunities of employment for him in the community. He helped his son Brian, who runs a small garage in the neighbourhood of Coronation Street.

In his attempt to grasp the essential generic features of soap opera, or at least those of the American daytime serial, Robert Allen explains the disproportionately high number of characters with middle-class professional identities in those serials (compared to their share of the US population) by the soap opera prerequisite of talk and social interaction. According to Allen, middle-class environments cater for those prerequisites more than working-class settings.

This, however, causes a dilemma in a programme such as *Coronation Street* which set out to feature life in a working-class community.

That is why the programme has made an effort to not only feature the odd worker and characters who are at least of working-class origin but to also integrate an industrial work sphere into the serial neighbourhood.

That effort is concentrated on the women who work in Mike Baldwin's denim factory (in the early days of the programme it used to be a rain coat factory that fulfilled the same function), which is situated well within the *Street*.

However, the work situation in Baldwin's factory is 'domesticated' to a point that it can but be called a trivialized representation of even a small-scale industrial entreprise. The workshop rather resembles a sewing-room where the women are mostly shown at the beginning or end of a working day or in breaks, or when they casually stop their sewing-machines in between. This is to say they are shown whenever there is an opportunity for them to talk.

Mike Baldwin's office is near the workshop in a glass box. It is behind that transparent 'walls' where Baldwin manages the factory and surveys his workforce.

On a symbolical level Baldwin's position is ambiguous. As it suggests on the one hand that he is a watch-dog or even an exploiter. But on the other hand it seems to express a certain corporate identity of workers and employer. For, naturally ups and downs in the factory's balance tend to quickly seep through to the women. Usually, their reactions to such knowledge are very fast. They either demand higher payment or start worrying about their jobs.

The years of the recession seem not to have affected Mike Baldwin's factory in any severe way. Nevertheless, he quite often referred to it, but mainly to prevent his female work-force from becoming too demanding.

Baldwin is often seen rebuking his workers for being unreliable, unpunctual, doing sloppy work and gossiping too much, but quite often the women retaliate with an onslaught of Lancashire temperament. In some sense the arguments in Baldwin's factory resemble more major domestic strifes than real labour disputes.

It is a conspicuous feature of those arguments that although Mike Baldwin objectively has much more power than the women and is not a soft person either, he only just manages to face up to their sharp Lancashire tongues.

The women seem to deal with him on equal terms rather than from a deferential position. This is especially the case when they meet Mike Baldwin in the 'Rover's Return', which unlike the factory seems to be neutral territory where everybody has the same right to be.

Incidentally, the undeferential behaviour of workers towards their employer is retained as a convention with the manager of the new supermarket who, like Mike Baldwin and everybody else in the serial, drinks his beer in the 'Rover's Return'. The supermarket opened in 1989 as part of the *Street's* modernisation process, introducing into the programme some of the images of the so-called Thatcher economic boom of the late eighties with its emphasis on business and management principles.

With Mike Baldwin, the programme always has seemed to be designed in such a way that in the final analysis not Baldwin with his thrusting business-man manner is allowed to take over the *Street*, but rather that he is taken over by the neighbourliness.[9] A factor which has invariably impaired Mike Baldwin's position in the frame of reference of the serial, with its outspoken claim to being northern, is his Cockney origin, which automatically puts him into the role of an outsider. Sometimes it seems as if the fact that he is from the South has made him more suspicious to the others in the *Street* than the fact that he belongs to the capital-owning class.

On some occasions, however, the tensions between him and his workers have resulted in more than just the ordinary clashes - namely in strikes.
Richard Paterson and John Stewart analyse a sequence of episodes broadcast in 1978 which deal with a strike in Baldwin's factory.
The information given by the two authors at first sight suggests that the strike episodes seem to deal with a rather genuine and realistic labour dispute: The female workforce of a small-scale factory come out on strike in solidarity with a colleague who has been dismissed. The dispute is sustained over a fictional time of two weeks and is featured in six episodes. The event obviously culminates in the fifth and sixth episodes when Baldwin attempts to bring in non-union labour despite the strikers' picketing outside the factory gate. This results in let-down minibus tyres and a smashed window. When the blackleg workers realise that they have been brought in as strike-breakers, they refuse to do the work. However, Mike Baldwin persuades them to stay inside the factory, so that the striking women outside believe that the strike- breakers are working. Eventually, the police are called by other residents of the *Street*, upon which the non-union workers can leave the factory. Subsequently, Ivy Tilsley negotiates with Baldwin as representative of the strikers. Baldwin gives in to the women's demand that their dismissed colleague be reemployed. Paterson and Stewart infer that there are some references in the strike episodes which relate the event to strikes in the real world. The two authors suggest:

> "Once the police sergeant is inside the factory the exchange with Mike Baldwin refers to an assumed knowledge of the 'real world' (the bitter strike at the Grunwick factory in London, etc.).[10]

At second sight, however, the strike appears much less realistic, for the event is obviously moulded into the conventions of the soap opera genre. As is mostly the case in soap opera, the strike, like any other event, seems to be rooted in pers-

---

[9] cf. Marion Jordan, op. cit., p. 35.

[10] Richard Paterson and John Stewart, Street Life. In Richard Dyer et al., op. cit., pp. 81-98, pp. 93/94.

onal reasons (e.g. the fiery personalities of some of the women) rather than different class interests.

Besides, the immediate cause which sparks off the strike appears rather trivial. For, it is Hilda Ogden (who within the frame of reference of the serial was then established mainly as a comic figure), who is dismissed from her job as a cleaner in the factory on the grounds of her demanding a new brush. On top of that, the whole strike is made to appear questionable by the fact that Hilda Ogden secretly accepts a new job (which the viewers know) while her former colleagues are on strike on her behalf.

In addition, the strike theme, which despite Hilda Ogdens's involvement in it, is still a serious enough topic, is counterbalanced by other more comic plots alternating with the strike storyline. In one of the funnier storylines Fred Gee, the barkeeper in the 'Rover's Return', is courting Alma Walsh but eventually decides not to propose to her because 'she is too bossy'. In fact the gender conflict expressed in male complaints about the bossiness of women versus female complaints about the selfishness of men appears in some of the other story-lines.

As is a strong convention in *Coronation Street*, these stories can be perceived as not only counterbalancing the strike theme but as also reflecting upon it. Here it is the gender relation or conflict, which is also part of the labour dispute between Baldwin and his female workforce, which are reflected.

As has been indicated elsewhere, soap opera in general has traditionally always had a prerogative of female characters. But while in the American serials women have been largely portrayed either as virtuous, weak or bitchy, *Coronation Street* has featured female characters, who - partially due to their working-class identity - are to varying degrees at the same time, assertive, strong, warm-hearted and still exploited by men.[11]

The centrality of women in soap opera in general, affects in *Coronation Street* that women are often in a stronger position than men. "Men are a pain in the neck"[12] used to be a standard phrase of Elsie Tanner's, which she also employs in one of the strike episodes.

Yet, the strong position of women in these particular episodes and in the serial in general, seems not to go as far as to question their roles as housewives and mothers. Rather, their position of strength is built up within these roles. Paterson and Stewart describe a scene in the Kabin, the newspaper shop in one of the streets adjacent to *Coronation Street*. There the spinsterly shop assistant, Mavis, talks endlessly about how much she adores children, whereupon Deirdre Langdon

---

[11] It is interesting to note at this point that Sonia Livingstone in her research on soap opera viewers found out that femininity in *Coronation Street* was allocated by the viewers to a different space than psychological gender stereotyping theories would normally presume. Thus, feminity in CS was not related to irationality, softness or weakness but to more matriarchal categories, eg. related to maturity, warmth, centrality to the community and sociability, in contrast to the rather more cold and childish masculinity of the male characters. (cf. Sonia Livingstone, Viewers' Interpretation of Soap Opera Characters. In: Philipp Drummond and Richard Paterson (eds.), *Television and Its Audience: International Research Perspectives*, (London, 1988).

[12] Richard Paterson and John Stewart, Street Life, p. 92.

(later Barlow) replies:

> "You don't know the half of it, all the cleaning and feeding, and seeing to, and the worry, starting with whether there is anything wrong with her, to whether something's going to happen to her (...)"[13]

Yet, the outcome of that conversation is that "despite the problems of motherhood and a forgetful husband she is 'lucky'."[14]

Other storylines which balance the strike theme and reflect upon aspects of it, deal with the community of *Coronation Street*. There is one plot in particular which counterbalances the disrupting effect of the strike in the *Street* community. That story deals with the inhabitants of the *Street* wanting to donate money for a new bed for Ena Sharples, who has been in hospital because of back pains. Ena Sharples does not want help from the Social Security because she is still from the old world and calls such help "charity". That is why the self-help system of the *Street* community has to be activated.

As the labour dispute grows fiercer it seems to become too strong to be counterbalanced or even solved within the ranks of the community. There has to be help from outside. That is to say the police have to be called. According to Paterson and Stewart, this is in disregard of the inside/outside opposition which is an underlying pattern of the serial. The two authors infer:

> "Annie takes the initiative in solving the problem by phoning for the police - outsiders, but agents of order."[15]

But before Mike Baldwin, the Cockney, has already crossed that borderline when bringing in workers from outside the community. Paterson and Stewart point out:

> "It is interesting that these women are marked as outsiders not only to the street (though two of them were former Baldwin employees before they were d ismissed), but also to the region. The chief spokeswoman has a distinct Geordie accent."[16]

As the strike seems to have been presented more like a major strife in the neighbourhood, trade unions apparently have no role in that labour dispute, except that the women who Baldwin has brought in from outside, are referred to as non-union labour.
The two authors also mention graffiti on the factory wall: a Swastika and a Hammer and Sickle. According to them, these drawings become images of right-wing and left-wing extremism.

---

[13] Richard Pater son and John Stewart, Street Life, p. 92.

[14] ibid.

[15] ibid., p. 93.

[16] Richard Paterson and John Stewart, op. cit., p. 93.

Paterson and Stewart find evidence in the narrative which seems to suggest a connection between the striking women and those symbols. Especially, the sequence in which the striking women are shown discussing Mike Baldwin's offer outside the factory gate reflects, according to Paterson and Stewart, dominant media representations of strikes at that time.

"The women are shown in a rabble, and Muriel, the one who wants to stay out (...), makes her vote with a Nazi salute."[17]

That incident seems to impart a wider political - and ideological dimension to the episodes, one which is clearly marked by a bias against striking workers. The opinion that strikes, especially if they occur as frequently as in the 70s, are socially disruptive and economically damaging was shared by a large proportion of people in Britain.
In the episodes analysed it is Mike Baldwin who expresses this widely held attitude when telling his workers:

"(..) But just remember one thing. There aren't any winners in a situation like this. Only losers. Lost production, lost orders, lost profits, lost pay, lost goodwill. And where are we now? Back exactly where we were before it started."[18]

However, though this statement sounds like a straight anti-union comment it has to be taken into account that it is Mike Baldwin who makes it, a character whose position within the frame of reference of the serial is ambiguous. That is why Paterson and Stewart are still able to conclude:

"What this analysis of two episodes brings out in particular is the variety of positions constructed for the viewer. No one set of attitudes and values is privileged in terms of dialogue, but a range of often contradictory positions is offered by the different characters working through the major oppositions."[19]

Nevertheless, it seems to be part of the underlying structure of the programme that the class aspect is mitigated. As for the strike, Paterson and Stewart suggest at one point that "the gender opposition is mapped on class oppositions".[20] Through its emphasis on the domestic and the parochial, the serial modulates the significance of the strike in such a way that the class dimension becomes secondary. Whereas, the gender opposition and the disruption of the community, caused by the strike become primary aspects of the event.
Besides, the overall set-up of the programme blurs the category of social class by presenting mainly characters from the 'respectable working class' and the petty bourgeoisie. These characters represent the large and ill-defined mass of 'common

---

[17] ibid., p. 96.

[18] ibid.

[19] Paterson and Steward, op. cit., p. 97.

[20] ibid. p. 86.

people', an image of the working class to which the programme seems to held always a strong affinity. What this image excludes, however, is the concept of working-class people as class-conscious members of political organizations, which, as, the long-term miners' strike in 1986/87 or the fierce boycott of Rupert Murdoch's plant in Wapping proved, was, in the first half of the Thatcher era and before, still a part of British reality.

4.2.   The Impact of 'The Affluence Debate'

Dorothy Hobson who in her book on *Crossroads* also briefly refers to *Coronation Street*, suggests:

"Coronation Street claims to reflect 'working-class culture', and it is strongly rooted in the traditional cultural working-class values of the 1950s period. In some respects the series (sic) is still located in the period of the early 60s when it began. "[21]

The years between 1953 and 1964, paradoxically the years of Conservative government were generally experienced as a time of transition for the working class in Britain. Those years have been termed 'years of affluence', for they mark the coming about of the post-war boom in Britain. That meant relatively full employment, an improved quality of work through technical innovations and shorter working hours, and a general decrease in poverty and want, partially due to the newly established welfare system.
The majority of working-class people experienced a change in their life-styles brought about by higher income and access to consumer goods, which for many included a television set.

Further changes were brought about through educational reforms, which provided working-class children with more access to higher education, though only a minority actually achieved it. In addition, new housing policies aimed at increasing owner-occupation, suburbanization and the redevelopment of the inner cities. Consequently, many streets like *Coronation Street*, or perhaps a few grades lower in standard, were demolished during that time. In the 1970s Trevor Blackwell describes the city of Blackburn, which is not far from Manchester, and in retrospect assesses the impact of the 1950s on the transformation of the traditional scenery of working-class life in the North:

"From the early nineteenth century up to the 1950s Blackburn was one of the most important Lancashire cotton towns, with some 90 per cent of its adult population working in the cotton and allied trades at the turn of the century. Factory chimneys still dominate a hard, hilly, windy town, with rows of terraced houses, interspersed with Twaites' pubs, fish and chips shops, small corner-shops, and more occasional chapels.

---

[21] Dorothy Hobson, *Crossroads: The Drama of A Soap Opera*, (London, 1982), p.32.

Since the 1950s a newer Blackwell has emerged, with white-tiled shopping precincts, a new technical college, an enlarged cathedral and high-rise flats. "[22]

The change in the working-class conditions of life, which entailed changes in life-styles and attitudes, gave rise to 'the embourgeoisement thesis' and subsequently to the affluence debate. The focal point of that debate which was largely restricted to intellectual circles was the concept (largely American in origin) that working-class people who enjoyed greater affluence would gradually assimilate to a middle-class way of life. Some participants in the debate interpreted that development in a positive way, while others were more critical.

With the latter it was mainly the decline or loss of the traditional working-class neighbourhood that was often considered as a threat to what many saw as the distinct culture of the working class, a culture that had developed particularly in the years of the depression during the 1930s and had helped people to survive.

In search of empirical evidence of the declining sense of togetherness amongst working-class people Peter Willmott and Michael Young, for instance, conducted a study on the changing kinship relationships of London working-class people. The investigation was designed as a comparative study of the situations before and after re-housing. The following two quotations from interviews of Willmott and Young with some of the people who had been moved from Bethnal Green in the East End of London to a new estate on the outskirts of the city illustrate some of the changes.

> "(...) In Bethnal Green you always used to have a little laugh on the doorstep. There's none of that in Greenleigh. (...) The neighbours round here are very quiet. They all keep themselves to themselves. They all come from the East End but they all seem to change when they come down here."[23]
> "In one interview the husband was congratulating himself on having a house, a garden, a bath-room and a TV - the tellie is a bit of a friend down here."[24]

A similar sense of the loss of traditional features of working-class life is expressed in Richard Hoggart's book *The Uses of Literacy* (1957). Hoggart's approach, however, is a different one. He is less concerned with the geographical transplantation of the working-class neighbourhood than with changes in the traditional working-class cultural values and beliefs. Accoring to him, working-class life and lore was being undermined by the increasingly shallow products of an Americanized commercial mass culture. Hoggart suggests:

> "(...) that we are moving towards the creation of a mass culture; that the remnants of what was at least in parts an urban culture 'of the

[22] Trevor Blackwell, "The History of a Working-Class Methodist Chapel", *Working Papers in Cultural Studies 5* (Spring 1974), pp. 65-83, p. 66.

[23] Michael Young and Peter Willmott, *Family and Kinship in East London*, ((Penguin) Harmondsworth, 16th ed., 1980), p. 147.

[24] ibid p. 147.

people' are being destroyed; and that the new mass culture is in some important ways less healthy than the often crude culture it is replacing."[25]

Critics have seen a link between the working-class culture Hoggart describes and analyses in his book and the milieu that is represented in *Coronation Street*.
This is particularly true of the first part of Hoggart's book, in which he draws on his boyhood experience in Hunslet, Leeds.
The similarities between the account in Hoggart's book and especially the early episodes of the serial written by Tony Warren are manifested on different levels.

Firstly, there are passages in the early scripts of the serial that correspond almost word by word with Hoggart's descriptions.
The first episode of *Coronation Street*, for example, contains one scene which deals with the relationship between grocers and the other people in the neighbourhood. In that scene Mrs. Lappin who up to then managed the corner shop in Coronation Street but has handeld it over to Florence Lena Lindley, explains her policy of giving credit to costumers.

> Mrs. Lindley: "What happens if they ask me for tick?"
> Mrs. Lappin : "I used to have a notice up there. 'Please Do Not Ask For Credit As A Refusal Often Offends'
> Mrs. Lindley: "Where's it gone?"
> Mrs. Lappin :"They asked just the same, so I took it down. It's in the back. But a bit on the slate's not a bad thing. If you don't let some of them have it, they wouldn't spend nearly as much (...)"[26]

A similar reference is contained in the *Uses of Literacy*. There Hoggart writes:

> "Newcomers may pin to the shelf at the back of the counter one of those notices which local jobbing printers produce, 'Please Do Not Ask For Credit As A Refusal Might Offend', but whether the notice stays up or not most of them have to start giving 'tick' before long."[27]

But more than textual parallels, it is the basic concept of the working-class community and milieu which *Coronation Street* seems to owe to *The Uses of Literacy*.

With reference to the improved living conditions of the working class after the War, Hoggart suggests:

> "(...) working-class people probably do not feel themselves to be members of a 'lower' group as strongly as they did a generation or two ago. Yet, those I have in mind still to a considerable extent retain a sense of

[25] Richard Hoggart, *The Uses of Literacy* ((Penguin) Harmondsworth, 9th ed., 1968), p. 24.

[26] The Text of the *First Episode of Coronation Street*, TV Times Souvenir Album, 1981.

[27] Richard Hoggart, op. cit., p. 61.

being in a group of their own (...)"[28]

It is evident that the apparently 'natural' but not particularly hostile feeling of being in a group of one's own corresponds to the sense of community which is reflected in *Coronation Street*.

Similar to Willmott and Young's study, Hoggart's description and analysis centres upon the working-class neighbourhood and family. These are, according to him, the most important generators of the working-class culture. What Hoggart, however, leaves out or at least neglects are the impact of the sphere of work and working-class political organisations on the working-class culture. Evidently, such a parochial concept of working-class culture matches the generic requirements of the soap opera narrative structure.

In addition, Hoggart's account, like *Coronation Street*, is based on an unrigorous definition of the working class. Hoggart stresses, for instance, that in terms of culture the boundaries between the working class and sections of the lower middle class are fluid. For that reason he proposes the concept of an 'urban culture of the people'[29]. Hoggart's description of the cultural group with which he is dealing resembles the inhabitants of Coronation Street. According to Hoggart,

"most of the employed inhabitants of these areas work for a wage, not a salary, and the wage is paid weekly; most have no other sources of income. Some are self employed; they may keep a small shop for members of the group to which culturally they belong or supply a service to the group, for example, as a 'cobbler', 'barber', 'grocer', 'bike-mender' or 'cast-off clothing dealer'."[30]

Hoggart also draws on the subtle distinctions which the inhabitants of the working-class neighbourhood make within the community.

"To the inhabitants there is a fine range of distinctions in prestige from street to street. Inside the single street there are elaborate differences of status, of standing', between the houses themselves; this is a slightly better house because it has a separate kitchen, or is at the terrace end, has a bit of a yard, and is rented at ninepence a week more. There are differences of grade between the occupants; this family is doing well because the husband is a skilled man and there is a big order in at the works; the wife here is a good manager and very houseproud, whereas the one opposite is a slattern."[31]

In the first episode of *Coronation Street* newcomer Mrs. Lappin (and the viewer)[32] is also introduced to 'the fine range of distinctions' in the *Street*. She soon

---

[28] ibid., p. 20.

[29] Hoggart derived the concept of the 'urban culture of the people' from T.S. Elliot's concept of a 'folk culture'.

[30] Richard Hoggart, op. cit., p. 20.

[31] Richard Hoggart, op. cit., p. 21.

[32] Incidentally, the device of introducing the audience to the serial world through the eyes of a newcomer was also adopted in the first episode of *Lindenstraße* on 8 December 1985. That episode featured Elfie and Siggie, a young unmarried couple, who moved into a flat in Lindenstraße and

meets Ena Sharples who makes it quite clear that she thinks everybody outside the *Street* pretentious and unreliable.[33] Thus, she dismisses the objectively near but subjectively foreign Esmerelda Street, where Mrs. Lindley lived before, by declaring:

"Esmerelda Street, eh? Very bay-window down there, aren't they? Oh, well, you'll find it very different up here."[34]

But Mrs. Lappin (and the viewer) soon gets to know the subtle distinctions inside Coronation Street. The first episode mainly focuses on the contrast between the Tanners and the Barlows.

Elsie Tanner - her husband absconded when her two children were small - is presented as the female head of a constantly quarreling family. Elsie, who works in a department store, is not particularly houseproud, but feckless and 'more of a slattern'. Her daughter Linda, a proper 'Lancashire lass', who is married to a Polish man but cannot get on with him, has just fled back to the maternal hearth, where she is accommodated again by Elsie with a somewhat grumbling sense of maternity and female solidarity.

Elsie's son Dennis has just returned from borstal and cannot find work, which causes frequent quarrels between him and his sharp-tongued mother.

The Barlows differ from the Tanners in many respects. They are a complete family of mother, father and two grown-up lads. The family could be grouped under the traditional label 'respectable working class'. Father Frank, a post-office worker, is less inclined than his wife to adopt middle-class standards. Thus, he insists on eating in shirt-sleeves and mends a bike in the middle of the living-room. There exists a permanent and for most of the time only barely suppressed tension between Frank Barlow and his eldest son, Ken, who is a 'scholarship boy' and studies at Manchester university. Ken is "directly critical of the details of their life - sauce and pre-buttered bread -and implicitly ashamed of his family -(...)"[35] Frank fully enacts the aggressive working-class father, hurt in his pride, when Ken informs his parents that he will be meeting a girl from a middle-class area at the Imperial Hotel. The choice of that dating place infuriates Ken's father because it is not only socially and economically distant from his circles but is also the very hotel where Ken's mother works in the kitchen to supplement the income of the family.

Frank Barlow seems to feel closer to his younger son, David, who is more like a real 'working-class lad'. He works in a garage (later he will start a career as professional footballer), his most ardent desire is to get a motor bike and his way of dressing is influenced by the MOD style, which was adopted by many working-

---

gradually got to know their new neighbours.

[33] Text of First Episode TV Times Souvenir Album, 1981.

[34] *Teaching Coronation Street* (BFI Educational Department, London 1983) p. 31.

[35] *Teaching Coronation Street* (BFI Educational Dep., London, 1983), p.30.

class youngsters during that period.

It is particularly interesting to note the juxtaposition of the three young men in the first episode of the serial: Ken Barlow, the scholarship boy, David BarIow, the hearty working-class youngster who is satisfied in his own class, and Dennis Tanner, the troublesome working-class brat and ex-borstal boy.

The scholarship boy is, partially for autobiographical reasons, also a concern of *The Uses of Literacy*. Hoggart infers that the scholarship boy pays for the benevolence received from the State by becoming uprooted from his original class. According to Hoggart, "he is at the friction-point of two cultures."[36]

Other parallels between *The Uses of Literacy* and the first episode of *Coronation Street* could be seen in the folk wisdom and common sense of which Hoggart gives an ample account in his book, and which particularly the older characters in the serial displayed.

Furthermore, it is striking to read Hoggart's description of a typical working-class living-room and consider that most living-rooms in *Coronation Street* until the mid-eighties still resembled that description (it should be remembered that most scenes are set in living-rooms).

> "(...) I should say that a good 'living-room' must provide three principal things: gregariousness, warmth and plenty of good food. The living-room is the warm heart of the family and therefore often slightly stuffy to a middle-class visitor. It is not a social centre but a family centre; little entertaining goes on there or in the front room, if there happens to be one; you do not entertain in anything approaching the middle-class sense."[37]

Yet, despite the striking parallels between the world depicted in *Coronation Street* and Richard Hoggart's account in *The Uses of Literacy*, there are also significant deviations from the book, due to the soap opera narrative structure, the entertainment function of the programme and its time of broadcast during early prime   time.

Thus, despite Hoggart's unrigorous definition of the working class, he seems to take it for granted that the core of the cultural group to which he refers is composed of the industrial working class. Whereas, the serial seems to have for the most part featured characters who, according to their occupational status, belong to the group which Hoggart describes as "culturally belonging" to the industrial working class.

A second deviation from Hoggart's account, in the early episodes of the serial, occoured in the relationship between men and women. For, though Hoggart stresses that the working-class mother plays a central role in the family, he also infers that she is likely to have a deferential relationship with her husband, who

---

[36] Richard Hoggart, op. cit., p. 292.

[37] ibid., p. 4.

may be aggressive and assertive in his role as main breadwinner.

> "(..) the working-class father (...) is the master in his own house'. This he is by tradition, and neither he nor his wife would want that changed. She will often refer to him before others as 'Mr. W' or 'the mester (...) In either case, there is likely to be a deference to him as the main breadwinner and heavy worker, even though these assumptions are not always correct today."[38]

Coronation Street seems to have always reflected mainly the last half of the last sentence. For the women in the serial have seldom shown deference to the men.

A third deviation from Hoggart's book seems to be the treatment of sex and talk about it in the serial. In contrast to the dominant middle-class moral code of the time, Hoggart writes about the attitude of working-class people to sex:

> "I do not mean to suggest, in relating these incidents, that working-class people are sexually more licentious than others: I think it doubtful whether they are. But sexual matters do seem nearer the surface, and sexual experience in the working classes is probably more easily and earlier acquired than in other social groups."[39]

In contrast to that, it has,always belonged to the image of the serial as a family programme that sex, though frequently alluded to, has never really been shown openly. Neither has the serial adopted the rough talk about sex, "the way many working-class men speak when no women are present"[40], which Hoggart observed on some occasions.
Afterall there have never been many occasions "when no women are present", which would have allowed an exploration of the 'coarser' layers of working-class men in *Coronation Street*.

The same could be said of fights and violence, which Hoggart suggests as a rather common feature of working-class life, particularly of the "truely slummy areas".[41] *Coronation Street* with its respectable working-class characters, which has never fallen into that category, has traditionally shown only relatively minor outbursts of temper which occasionally included punches and beating. The more recent proneness of the serial to include violence cannot be interpreted in the light of social documentary. Rather, it has to be attributed to developments in the soap opera genre which affect an increased us of cop-and-robber violence.

A further deviation in the serial from the milieu described by Hoggart, was the low number of children. While Hoggart infers that working-class families al-

---

[38] Richard Hoggart, op. cit., p. 54.

[39] ibid., p. 98.

[40] ibid., p. 91.

[41] Richard Hoggart, op. cit., p. 90.

Scholarshipboy Ken and his parents Frank and Ida Barlow in the 1st episode

Elsie Tanner and her son ex-borstal boy Dennis rowing over money in the 1st episode

John Osborne: *Look Back in Anger*

most invariably had many children, the serial - due to the difficulty of including young children in a continuous production - for a long time did not feature many children. In the early days this deficit was made up by a standard shot in the opening sequence that depicted a crowd of children playing and chanting nursery rhymes. Only the recent refurbishment of the serial due to competition with other soap operas, has led to an increase in the number of children and adolescents who are actually featured.

4.3.   The New Realism in Literature, Drama and Film

Another factor in the cultural climate during the early days of *Coronation Street* was the 'New Realism' that became the predominant mode of representation on the stage, in the novel and also in film. It had developed partially as a reaction against the highly intellectual and partially experimental literature and drama of the main writers of the 1930s and their post-war successors.
In retrospect the era of the New Realism is often described as having been sparked off by the performance of John Osborne's play *Look Back in Anger* (1957) at the Royal Court Theatre, London. Alexander Walker suggests:

> "Jimmy Porter's outburst or rage against life, class and society in May 1956 sundered all that stifling atmosphere of socially deferential conservatism which had settled over Britain since the early fifties."[42]

In reference to the title of Osborne's play, critics coined the name 'Angry Young Men' and used it as a label for dramatists and writers whose works emerged parallel or subsequent to *Look Back in Anger* and likewise reflected anger, indignation or only irritation.
But the 'tacky' label which reflects the attempt to apply a group name the numerous representatives of that artistic movement, cannot conceal that it was really a very heterogeneous group.
What many shared, however, was a sense of being uprooted from society, or more particularly from their social class, and a dissatifaction with existing intellectual norms.
In addition, the majority of them had in common that they had been brought up in working-class - or lower middle-class families in provincial cities. Most of them had acquired higher education and academic distinctions with the aid of the scholarship system. Some of them, like Shelagh Delaney who incidentally was raised in Salford, did not even receive a higher education.
Many representatives of the New Realism made a deliberate choice to present characters with working-class - or at least lower-class backgrounds in their novels and plays. That gave their works a Social Realist quality.
In the theatre, the term 'kitchen sink drama' came into current use, mainly

---

[42] Alexander Walker, *Hollywood England: The British Film Industry in The Sixties*, (London, 1974) p. 41.

associated with the works of such dramatists as John Osborne, Alun Owen, Arnold Wesker or Shelagh Delaney. It was used to describe plays which "metaphorically (or psychologically) and in some cases literally centred on the kitchen sink."[43] Buckman sees a link between the tradition of the 'kitchen sink drama' and 'the flattened and mundane reality' of British soap operas.

Among the novelists who adhered to the new Social Realist tendency were such writers as Alan Sillitoe, Sid Chaplin, David Storey, Stan Barstow and numerous others.

The new trend had a surprisingly broad reception by the public, especially as many of the novels and plays were made into films by directors like Tony Richardson, Karel Reisz, Jack Clayton, John Schlesinger and others. Surprisingly, those films proved extremely successful in the commercial cinema. In addition, television, especially the newly established commercial channel with Granada in the vanguard, eager to earn prestige, revealed itself as a new force in the publication of that trend.

The fact that people from all strata of society read the books, saw the plays and, particularly the films, evoked for some time "an almost universal interest in the affairs of the working class totally new in the history of working-class literature".[44] *Coronation Street* in some respects constitutes a spill-over of that trend into a popular television genre.

A comparison between *Coronation Street* and the Social Realist literature and drama, however, is only possible in some key aspects. One such aspect is, for instance, the use of local accents and dialects as an important factor in the presentation of a working-class milieu.

The characters in Alan Sillitoe's novel *Saturday Night and Sunday Morning*, for instance, converse in Nottingham dialect and live in a working-class neighbourhood which resembles the one represented in *Coronation Street*.

But in contrast to the serial, Sillitoe's novel naturally concentrates on the presentation of an individual character, Arthur Seaton. Athur Seaton and other men in the novel, unlike most men in the serial, are distinguished by their tough masculinity and sexual frankness. Whereas, the female characters in the novel, unlike those in the serial, seem to be subservient to the aggressive men, though their working-class upbringing makes them less inhibited than middle-class women.

In Shelagh Delaney's plays *A Taste of Honey* and *The Lion in Love*, which are set in or near Manchester, characters' accents resemble those in *Coronation Street*. Also other aspects compare with the serial. Thus, in both plays women are as central as in the serial. The women in *The Lion in Love*, like most of the women

---

[43] J.A. Cuddon, *A Dictionary of Literary Terms*, edited by J.A. Cuddon, ((Penguin) Harmondsworth, 1977), pp. 351-352.

[44] Ingrid von Rosenberg, "Militancy, Anger and Resignation: Alternative Moods in The Working-Class Novel of The 1950s and Early 1960s", in: H. Gustav Klaus (ed.), *The Socialist Novel in Britain: Towards The Recovery of A Tradition*, (Brighton, 1982), pp. 145-165, p. 147.

in the serial, are marked by assertive - and not very subservient manners.

While in her first play, *A Taste of Honey*, Shelagh Delaney does not give much scope to the presentation of a working-class neighbourhood, her second play, *The Lion in Love* is firmly set in such a neighbourhood and a system of kinship relations.

Besides, there are elements in the dramaturgical style of the two plays which seem to remind of a soap opera dramaturgy:

> "(...) the action counts for virtually nothing; rather do the fragments of plot serve as an excuse for us to examine these people, to see how they live together and to try and understand why they are as they are (...)"[45]

The dialogues in *The Lion in Love* have been described by critics as marked by a naturalistic, everyday quality, which again suggests a similarity with dialogues in *Coronation Street*.

John Russel Taylor suggests:

> "A lot of the writing here not only seems like the small exchange of unintelligent everyday conversation, but actually is just that, virtually untouched by the dramatist's art."

It is interesting that Taylor unintentionally proposes a soap opera filmic style to enliven the play. According to him, "it needs thickening" and "in some way the close-ups of television would help".[46]

Although, as suggested before, the numerous dramatists and writers who wrote Social Realist drama and novels were a very heterogeneous group, critics have in retrospect have made out a number of conventions which cristallized from the stream of Social Realist writing.

Thus, apart from a few Communist authors, the Social Realist writers of that time seem to have shown little concern for the political dimension of working-class life. Instead, most of them concentrate on the personal conflicts of their protagonists, which in many cases are presented as only indirectly rooted in the social conditions. Marion Jordan suggests the following summary of core features of the Social Realist novels and plays:

> "(...) though these events are ostensibly about *social* problems they should have as one of their central concerns the settling of people in life; that the resolution of these events should always be in terms of the effect of personal interventions; that the characters should be either working-class or the classes immediately visible to the working classes (shopkeeper, say or the two-man business) and should be credibly accounted for in terms of the 'ordinariness' of their homes, families, friends (...) that the style should be such as to suggest an unmediated, unprejudiced and complete view of reality; to give, in summary, the impression that the reader, or viewer, has spent some time at the ex-

---

[45] John Russell Taylor, *Anger and After*, (Fakenham, 1962), p. 136.

[46] ibid.

pense of the characters depicted.[47]

Jordan also stresses that some of these conventions could be easily merged with the rules of the soap opera format.
Coronation Street has outlived the cultural trend which was so dominant at the time of its inception. But some of its conventions, seem to be solidified in the underlying structure of the serial.[48]

4.4.   The Sense of Nostalgia in Coronation Street

The solidification of the realism of *Coronation Street* in the period of its commencement has for a long time sustained a rather old-fashioned face, which communicated a certain nostalgia.
During the first ten years or so the aesthetic codes of black-and-white television helped to stress the documentary tone of the serial. Besides, the scenery of the working-class terrace, the setting of the serial, was still more typical during those years than it is today. Marion Jordan who attempts to grasp the changes in the aesthetic codes of the serial - partially due to colour production but also due to the loss in typicality, suggests:

> "The early programme's shots behind the credit titles showed *Coronation Street* under a forbiddingly dark sky. Now the sun shines on it, as a cat curls up in contented sleep (finds, in other words, the comfort of home), and a tree blossoms in the back alley (signifying to us all the fragile beauty to be found in the most unlikely spots)."[49]

As a result of the recent transformation of the programme, colour and light have attained even a greater significance. The serial rarely contains the grim and depressing scenes shot in bad weather and under a bleak sky, by which it was still marked in the mid-eighies.

But the very setting of the old-fashioned street has really carried a sense of nostalgia for a long time. In fact, if the programme were to be realistic and typical again, at least realistic and typical in the already mitigated manner of the earlier years, the *Street* would either have to be demolished and the inhabitants featured in a new estate, or it would be more than half peopled by Pakistanis or West Indians.
However until very recently *Coronation Street* did not feature many characters from ethnic minorities. Several attempts to bring in a coloured family resulted in negative reactions from the viewers. Apparently, it was its 'intact Englishness' which constituted one of the programme's sources of attraction for a majority

---

[47] Marion Jordan, Realism and Convention. In: Richard Dyer et al., op. cit., p. 28.

[48] cf. Dorothy Hobson, op. cit. p. 32.

[49] Marion Jordan, op. cit., p. 35.

white audience. That implied that for a long time non-white characters appeared only as guest characters. Since the mid-eighties the programme regularly featured a black girl, Shirley Armitage, working in Mike Baldwin's factory. Shirley, however, was not a resident of Coronation Street but lived in one of the neighbouring streets. That changed, as part of *Coronation Street's* transformation, when in 1988 she moved into the flat above Alf Roberts' shop, together with her white boyfriend Curly Watts. Thus, *Coronation Street* featured an interracial romance even before *EastEnders* did this later in the same year. Subsequently, *Coronation Street* also introduced the character of an Asian student. But apart from that, there have up to now not been many characters from ethnic minorities in the serial. Instead, there seems to be a deliberate effort to show black faces among the extras who people the public places of the serial, such as the pub or the supermarket. Compared to a real neighbourhood and also in comparison with *EastEnders* the appearance of non-white residents in *Coronation Street* is kept at a rather low level.

Since the late seventies, the programme has paid some credit to the changing scenery of the city in the opening shots, depicting high-rise flats on the horizon behind the quarter with the apparently still endless rows of working-class terraces. But this only adds to the sentimentalizing tone of the opening sequence. For it conveys the impression of a threatened idyll.

Even in the early days, the programme always left out the poorer sides of working-class existence in the North, which never totally vanished and in fact re-emerged with the long-term economic crisis of the late seventies and early eighties. Instead, the programme seems to have adopted the image of the 'affluent worker' as a core concept and has throughout those years imperturbably continued to reflect that image, without, however, removing the workers from the traditional scenery of the socially intact neighbourhood to the isolation of modern city life.

Due to the recent transformation of the programme, it now belongs to its style that it not only contains the implicit concept of 'the affluent worker' from a bye-gone age in its deeper structure but that it much more explicitly displays an image of affluence in the outward appearances of its characters and their homes. Yet, the nostalgic undercurrent in the serial seems to set limits to the use of images which convey, for instance, the Thatcherite idea of affluence too massively. This became especially obvious in a 1990 storyline, in which Nigel Ridley, one of the brewery owners, contemplated turning the Rover's Return into an American-style theme pub. Landlady Bet Lynch refused to comply with such plans and in the end she was supported by Ridley's senior business partner Cecil Newton[50]. On such occasions the narrative includes conventional comic references playing upon the conventional old-fashioned character of the serial.

The nostalgic ethos seems to have been inherent to the programme already

---

[50] This causes the television critic of the *Times Saturday Review* (8 December 1990) to infer that "the Thatcher years really ended this summer with the parable of the Rover's Return".

from its beginning, despite the documentary tone of the early episodes, Thus, the signature tune composed by Eric Spier resembles the melody of *Thanks for the Memory*.[51]

A mythic/nostalgic quality in the image of working-class life as portrayed by *Coronation Street* is seen as early as 1962 by W.J. Weatherby. He compares the serial's view of working-class life to an experience in a slum clearance area, where a seventy-eight-year-old woman refused to leave her street which was doomed to demolition. Weatherby infers:

> "In her tales all was golden and warmhearted: the tragedies - of poverty, of sickness, of dead ends - were dimmed by nostalgia, the class bitterness muted in what had now become 'the good old days'."[52]

According to Weatherby, *Coronation Street*'s view of life in a back street seemed essentially the same as the old lady's.

Under a slowly changing contemporary layer, *Coronation Street* seems to have conveyed that image until today. In a way it has conserved the best of a disappearing working-class milieu, of which remnants still exist today, especially in the North of England, and - what is perhaps more important - of which many people still have memories.
But even people who do not have such memories, because they belong to a different class or even come from a different country, can still enjoy the essence of that milieu: the community spirit which can survive despite 'blows' from outside and despite controversies inside the neighbourhood.
Although that community spirit is featured among a set of 'urban common people', it is likely to have some national significance as well, in rememberance of the mythical 'national community' that 'once closed its ranks to resist the Blitz'.[53]

As time passes, it will be increasingly the essence of the community which counts rather than any realistic image of working-class life.

4.5.   Elements of Comedy in Coronation Street

In a 1974 *Guardian* interview *Coronation Street* ex-producer Suzie Hush stressed that apart from its claim to realism and the cumulative dramatic tradition,

---

[51] Marion Jordan, op. cit., p. 35.

[52] W.J. Weatherby, "Granada's Camino Real", *Contrast* (Summer, 1962), repr. in: Edward Buscombe (ed.) *BFI Dossier Number 9: Granada: The First 25 Years*, (London, 1981), pp. 79-88, p. 82.

[53] Characters referred to the sense of community during the years of the Blitz in the early years of the serial. One episode, in which the whole *Street* is evacuated to the Mission Hall because of a broken gas mains, is particularly obvious.

it is especially the comedy which has always marked the serial.[54] In fact it is the comedy which in the early years enlivened the sometimes drab realism and by which into now any stern nostalgia and melodramatic mood[55] is put into perspective.

In some ways it seems as if it is the comedy rather than the Social Realism which has always distinguished the programme in the international soap opera genre. This seems to become more true the longer the serial survives the cultural climate of its inception.
Marion Jordan suggests that the comic elements help to expose the 'artifice' of the conventions of the Soap Opera Realism.

In fact, the short linear syntagms, which are characteristic of soap opera narratives and which also mark *Coronation Street*, suggest a similarity with situation comedy. However, despite a number of common features, comic scenes in *Coronation Street*, unlike in situation comedy, do not explicitly aim at a punch line. Rather, the comic elements seem to be randomly strewn into otherwise realistic situations.
Jordan distiguishes between three major comic devices in Coronation Street: Caricature, comic dialogue and parody .

The use of character caricature as a source of comedy seems to be most natural in a genre in which character is as central as in soap opera and "which encourages background stereotyping with the foregrounding of particularities"[56] But the caricatures in *Coronation Street* have always been mislead with more realistic characters.

One of the most famous example of caricature used to be the character of Ena Sharples (she left the programme in the late seventies). According to Jordan, "Mrs. Sharples has always been treated in this way" from the moment of her aggressive self-introduction in the first episode: "I'm a widow woman".[57] Jordan infers: "There is nothing of Realism in the hugely square face or the large mesh hairnet clamped in place with metal pins" and even though the producers may have changed Ena Sharples over the years "from the acerbic comic eccentric to the infallible gnomic grandmother, but her style has always been that of a caricature."[58]

Unlike Ena Sharples, Annie Walker, the former landlady of the 'Rover's

---

[54] R. Thornber, "Why *Coronation Street* will never be the Susie Hush Show". *Guardian* 16.12. 1974, p. 8.

[55] The message of Len Fairclough's fatal accident', for instance, arrived when the residents of the *Street* were celebrating the Ogden's Ruby wedding.

[56] Marion Jordan, op. cit., p. 38.

[57] Marion Jordan, op. cit., p 37.

[58] ibid.

Return' with her pretentious leanings, used to be a more realistic character in the early days of the programme. Yet, in later years she became "increasingly written up into caricature".[59] She was depicted as an obviously semi-educated, pretentious, pompous and domineering person.

Hilda Ogden being notoriously nosey, bossy and vulgar, was another example of caricature in the serial. She used to be especially effective in juxtaposition to her, fat and obtuse husband Stan. Almost invariably she was depicted wearing a mac and curlers. In relation with her husband she often enacted the sterotype of the 'strident and easily excitable' wife. Her particular speciality were malapropisms, symptoms of her pretensions and lack of education. (One wall in the Ogden's living-room was decorated with a rather tasteless mural, depicting a swarm of flying seagulls, to which Hilda invariably referred as her 'murial'.)
Her husband Stan in his extraordinary shapelessness and obtuseness was certainly also a caricature, though less stylized than Hilda.

Until some years ago, the programme had a tendency to use only older characters as caricature[60]. But in more recent years there is at least one young character who clearly is a caricature. This is Curly (Norman) Watts, who with his thick specs, his straggly, straight hair and queer ideas was from the mid-eighties onwards featured as the young 'weirdo' of *Coronation Street*. Despite the fact, that Curly has several A-levels, he previously worked as binman and scrap dealer while devoting his spare time to queer interlectual hobbies. However, in 1987 he resumed his higher education and attended a business course at the polytechnic. Subsequently, he got a job as trainee manager in the newly opened supermarket and is now in suit and smarmed down hair a caricature Yuppy.

The second comic device: funny dialogue likewise suggests itself, since talking is so vital for the serial's narrative. Marion Jordan suggests:

"There is a Realist background dialogue of unremarkable commonplaceness but frequently the conversation erupts (...) into a stylised repartee, distinguished only by the class accents from that brittle West End social comedy (...)."[61]

Marion Jordan qualifies her comparison with the "brittle West End social comedy" by referring to "Eddie Yeat's comment on Mrs. Walker's claim to be fastidious that he is just as fast, not quite as 'ideous' (...)"[62] and to "Mrs. Sharples exchange (in the first episode) 'What religion are you then?' - 'I don't really know

---

[59] ibid.
   Incidentally, some of my English friends saw in her a parody of Mrs. Thatcher.

[60] cf. Marion Jordan, op. cit., p. 37.

[61] Marion Jordan, op. cit., p. 38.

[62] ibid.

much about it.' - 'Oh I see C of E. "[63]

However, *Coronation Street* also contains more vulgar comic dialogues employing the "language of the stand-up comic"[64].

Jordan presents the following examples:

> "The comic pattern is on the same lines but goes further with its suggestion of the straight man and the comic in encounters such as Ray's attempted pick-up: 'Why don't you sit down for a bit?' - 'A bit of what?'; or its use of deliberately vulgar double entendre in the manner of McGill postcards, as in Elsie's disclaimer: 'It might be some time since I last ran up a trouser leg'."[65]

The third comic device which, accoring to Jordan, is frequently used in the serial is parody. Thus, Eddie Yeats, who in many respects was a caricature already, sometimes parodied in a down-to-earth, vulgar manner a more eloquent character. Paterson and Stewart quote him calling himself "a gentleman of leisure"[66] in one of the strike episodes, during which he is unemployed. Bet Lynch, in her tight tiger-skin patterned dress, her peroxide blond upswept hairstyle and at least one surplus layer of make-up was "in the normal run of the programme a stereotype of the tarty barmaid (with of course a stereotypical heart of gold). She often enacted a parody of the type - offering her bosom or her company in a caricature of the common or promiscuous."[67]

Sometimes one character is used to parody another one. Thus, Hilda Ogden was often suggested as a parody of Mrs. Walker. Since, both of them were pretentious and tried to speak in an eloquent manner but Hilda's vulgarity was more obvious. Thus Mrs. Walker's pretentiousness was exposed trough Hilda displaying similar leanings.

In addition, entire narrative strands are parodied by other stories.

Marion Jordan gives an example:

> " (...) as when we move from Annie Walker's discussion of the merits of different forms of protein to Stan sitting over his meat and potato pie and baked beans."[68]

Sometimes, the whole set-up of the programme is parodied when characters, for instance, refer in a ridiculing manner to the isolation of *The Street* or to the unnatural culmination of dramatic events in sombody's life.

There are a number of comic traditions which seem to be reflected in

---

[63] ibid.

[64] ibid.

[65] ibid., p. 37.

[66] Paterson and Stewart, Street Life. In: Richard Dyer et al p. 85.

[67] Marion Jordan, op. cit., p. 38.

[68] ibid., p. 37.

Coronation Street. One such tradition is music hall comedy, a constituent of a past era of working-class - or rather popular culture in Britain (though more of the South than the North of England).[69]

That element, for example, seemed to be particularly obvious in one of the episodes which Susie Hush produced in 1975. The episode dealt with bar-maid Bet Lynch learning that her illegitimate son had been killed in a car accident while being a soldier in Northern Ireland. The overall atmosphere of that episode was serious but some 'comic relief' was brought about through the character of Eddie Yeats, at that time one of the *Street's* ne'er-do-wells with several prison and borstal sentences on his record. Shortly before, he had unsuccessfully courted Bet Lynch and in one scene of the episode in question he was complaining to Minnie Caldwell who then was his landlady, that he was fat and ugly and had no luck with women.

But his shapeless figure suggested him as a comic character, a caricature and when on top of that he started singing a song in typical music hall manner: 'they called me fat sow...', the scene in spite of all its vulgarity got a bitter-comic quality. The mixture of comedy and calamity expressed a certain stoical humour.

A more recent comic tradition that seems to have had an influence on the serial, are the Ealing comedies, which marked the British cinema between about 1949 and 1955.[70] But, according to Charles Barr, the influence of the Ealing film studios was still visible in TV productions of the late 1970s.[71] Like *Coronation Street*, the Ealing comedies had Realist settings and aimed at showing 'the people', which means they featured mainly petty bourgeois characters, small shop-keepers and clerks. One type of Ealing comedies rested on natural language and dealt with social disruption (instead of gags).

A comic tradition which is particularly stressed by Marion Jordan is that of the standup comic in the working-men's club in the North of England.

> "The comic routines (...) are at home, too, even in a Realist world, when the Realist world is that of the northern working class, (...) in whose well patronised working-men's clubs the standup comic (as likely as not a woman), whose stock-in-trade is the conversational ad lib, often with a a foot sitting (in mock Realist fashion) in the audience, traditionally makes a living."[72]

Jordan quite openly expresses her appreciation for the way in which the

---

[69] cf. Gareth Stedman Jones, "Working-Class Culture and Working Class Politics in London, 1870-1900: Notes On The Remaking Of A Working Class", in: Tony Bennett et al. (eds.), *Popular Culture: Past and Present*, (London, 1982), pp. 92-121.

[70] Ealing Studios were the first British sound studio in Britain built in 1931 and taken over by the BBC in 1955. The name 'Ealing' is most commonly associated with the comedies which were produced between 1949 and 1955.

[71] cf. Charles Barr, *Ealing Studios*, (London, 1977), p. 181.

[72] Marion Jordan, op. cit., p. 38.

Two of the long-standing older CS-characters: Ena Sharples (from 1960-1978) and Albert Tatlock (from 1960-1984)

Stan and Hilda Ogden, the couple with the most stable marriage in Coronation Street (they appeared in the serial together from 1963-1984)

Photos: British Film Institute

Former bar-maid Bet Lynch as 'respectable' landlady of the Rover's Return with husband Alec Gilroy in 1990

Photo: Granada Television

comic is used in the serial. According to her *Coronation Street* shares the same world-view as the northern club comic, who is "wryly aware that one may appear craggily foolish to the bland world outside and must therefore, hit out first."[73] In reference to the outdated Realism in the programme she suggests:

> "This kind of supposedly defensive fossil group may, in a programme like *Coronation Street*, twice weekly, celebrate its own virtues, and forestall attack by appearing to be its own most astute critic.[74]

4.6.   Elements of Camp in Coronation Street

The self-parody which is an occasional aspect of the programme constitutes a playful handling of conventions and narrative rules from within the programme. In addition, the programme by its longevity is likely to engender modes of reception which are marked by a playful handling also of such narrative elements which from within the programme are suggested as Realist. Such modes of reception, which refute a Realist reading of conventional Realist narratives, are likely to be part of what may be termed 'a postmodernist disposition' of the audience, which applies to different groups of viewers to varying degrees.[75]
One such mode of reception which refutes a Realist reading is the Camp vision which Susan Sontag defines as follows:

> "a certain mode of aetheticism. It is one way of seeing the world as an aesthetic phenomenon. That way, the way of Camp, is not in terms of beauty, but in terms of the degree of artifice, of stylization."[76]

'The Camp way of looking at things' transforms films and other objects which are originally intended as serious but have become over-conventionalized into objects of fun. Susan Sontag infers: "In naive or pure Camp, the essential element is seriousness, a seriousness that fails."[77]
From that point of view the serial seems to defy the 'Camp' label because of its elements of self-parody, which, as Marion Jordan thinks, suggest that the programme is aware of its 'artifice'. But Susan Sontag proposes a more subtle concept of camp.

> "Successful Camp - a movie like Carne's Drole de Drame; the film performances of Mae West and Everett Horton; the portions of the Goon Show - even when it reveals self-parody, reeks of self-love."[78]

---

[73] Marion Jordan, op. cit., p. 39.

[74] ibid.

[75] Since so far, however, postmodernist theory has not engendered many empirical studies of the audience, this can only be a theoretical postulation.

[76] Susan Sontag, *Against Interpretation (And Other Essays)*, (New York, 6. ed., 1966), p. 277.

[77] ibid., p. 283.

[78] Susan Sontag, *Against Interpretation (And Other Essays)*, New York, 6. ed., 1966), p. 282-283.

Coronation Street certainly 'reeks of self-love'. Since it has always been a 'cherished child' of its makers and as Marion Jordan infers, 'it forestalls attack by appearing to be its own most astute critic'. Besides, even self-parody can become stylized and conventionalized.

Moreover, *Coronation Street*, which like all soap operas, suggests that it portrays a 'parallel life' will appeal to the more detached searcher of Camp as an epitome of 'life as a theatre'.

In the past the Camp vision may have been brought about by some characters which were born Camp figures. The most obvious one was Bet Lynch when she still was the barmaid in her extravagantly styled dresses whith their strong not of the 60s. Apart from the tight tiger-skin patterned dress which she wore behind the bar, Bet also dressed herself in either close-fitting and short, or in puffed out, fluffy outfits of flashy colours. Susan Sontag stresses: "The hallmark of Camp is the spirit of extravagance.[79] With Bet Lynch it was a cheap extravagance, as befits the overall image of ordinariness which marks the serial. But it is not only her appearance that suggested Bet as a Camp figure but also her demeanour, which sometimes was marked (and still is) by a flirtatious display of sex-appeal, quick, sharp and at times cynical repartees and a certain air of wordly wisdom.

Susan Sontag points out: "What Camp taste responds to is 'instant character' (...) and, conversely, what it is not stirred by is the sense of the development of character."[80] *Coronation Street*, like any long-running serial with short episodes, relies on instant characterisation. Likewise, there is only limited - or at least inconsistent development of characters.

According to Susan Sontag, time is an important factor in bringing about a Camp vision towards certain objects.

> "Time may enhance what seems simply dogged or lacking in fantasy now because we are too close to it, because it resembles too closely our own everyday fantasies (...)
> It's simply that the process of aging or deterioration provides the necessary detachment - or arouses a necessary sympathy."[81]

However, with a serial like *Coronation Street* time is ambivalent in that respect. For, despite the solidifaction of the basic structure of the programme in the time of its inception, the programme-makers continue to insert fresh characters and new themes into that structure to suggest that it still features contemporary everyday life in the North of England.

---

[79] ibid., p. 286.

[80] Susan Sontag, *Against Interpretaion (And Other Essays)*, (New York, 6. ed., 1966), p. 286.

[81] ibid., p. 285.

5.　CLOSE-ANALYSIS OF THE TWO CORONATION STREET EPISODES OF 17 AND 21 FEBRUARY 1983

5.1.　The Context of The Two Episodes

Regular or occasional viewers of *Coronation Street* are familiar with the small-scale world of the *Street* with its atmosphere of homely or at times vulgar ordinariness.

Needless to say, the majority of viewers were also likely to be familiar with the long-standing characters who appear in the two episodes under consideration. Consciously or subconsciously, most of the spectators of these episodes without doubt were also accustomed to the rules of the *Coronation Street* narrative. It is within that context that the two episodes in question have to be analysed.

In their analysis of individual episodes of *Coronation Street* Richard Paterson and John Stewart draw the attention to the fact that prior to the introduction of any new narrative strand in the serial there already exists "such a large lexical myth-ology", "so that the text can operate on many different levels according to the knowledge of the viewer."[1]

The dominant theme of the episodes analysed is Deirdre and Ken Barlow's marital crisis, brought about by the revelation that Deirdre Barlow has an affair with factory owner Mike Baldwin.

The way in which the announcer introduces the first episode suggests that the audience have known of that affair and that it has already been discussed in the popular press.[2]

Deirdre Barlow's "sordid bit on the side",[3] as the cuckolded husband Ken Barlow puts it, has been a 'longterm cliffhanger' for quite a while. Hilary Kingsley talks of "a hugely enjoyable British newspaper hype that rivalled 'Dallas's Who Shot JR 'beat-up'". According to her, "a spellbound nation watched Deirdre meet Mike fur-tively behind Ken's back."[4]

---

[1]　Richard Paterson and John Stewart, op. cit., p. 98.

[2]　cf. for instance *The Daily Mail* of 6 February 1983.

[3]　cf. shooting transcript episode two, sequence: 8, scene 1.

[4]　Hilary Kingsley, op. cit., p. 93.

5.2.   Themes, Plots and Characters

5.2.1.   Themes

With regard to the following thematic analysis, it is important to bear in mind that
the two episodes under consideration are part of a long continuum. This implies
that the themes and storylines cannot be limited to these episodes only but stretch
out into previous and subsequent episodes. Besides, it should be taken into account that there may be themes present in the episodes, which but long-term
viewers are able to discern.

With those reservations in mind, the two episodes can be perceived as marked by
the ensuing thematic structure:

	1st episode	2nd episode
Ken's job	MT	
The Ken/Deirdre/Mike Crisis	P	MT
The Ogdens' financial problems	MT	ST
The Suzie/Marion/Elsie Crisis	MT	
Bet/Suzie/Fred relation	ST	ST
The relation men/women in general	P	
The return of Mrs. Walker		ST
Fred's car		P
Uncle Albert		P

MT = Main Theme   ST =   Secondary Theme   P = Theme Present[5]

It is noticeable that the first episode has three main themes, whereas the second
episode has only one: the Ken/Deirdre/Mike crisis which is only a 'theme present'
in the first episode.

5.2.2.   Plots

5.2.2.1.   The Ken/Deirdre/Mike Storyline

(1st episode)
Deirdre Barlow has been having an affair with factory-owner Mike Baldwin for
several weeks. Emily Bishop, Deirdre's moralistic, motherly friend and Mike
Baldwin's secretary, seems to be the only person who knows about it. Emily quite

---

5   This diagram draws on a similar diagram developed by Richard Paterson and John Stewart in:
     Street Life, op. cit., p. 83.

openly shows her disapproval to her boss and entreats Deirdre to terminate the affair. But Deirdre is not willing to listen to her advice.

Deirdre's husband Ken Barlow is rather depressed because he was not accepted for a job with the local Council. He asks Alf Roberts, the owner of the corner-shop, who is an elected Independent[6] member of the Council to find out why he was not accepted. Eventually, Alf manages to find out that the committee who is responsible for the appointments thought that Ken had not the appropriate qualifications for the job. But allegedly that was not the reason why they turned him down. Rather, it was his apparent lack of vigour and enthusiasm which was the decisive factor. Alf confides what he found out to Deirdre, who works as assistent in the corner-shop.

At first Deirdre hesitates to tell Ken what she heard from Alf. However, in the course of a conversation, in which Ken displays a rather fatalistic attitude, it slips out. When their discussion becomes more heated Deirdre also confronts Ken with the fact that she has a relationship with Mike Baldwin. Ken is shocked.

(2nd episode)
Ken and Deirdre spend the next day attempting to talk about their marriage, but each time they end up rowing. Deirdre reproaches Ken with not really sharing his life with her instead she thinks he "tolerates her like a piece of furniture". Ken is embittered by Deirdre's deceit and the callousnes with which she concealed her affair.
The domestic crisis at the Barlows' culminates in Mike Baldwin's coming to their house. It comes to a scuffle at the door, in the course of which Ken loses his nerves and takes Deirdre by the throat. Deirdre breaks down crying.

Only after some time do they resume their conversation, which, however, ends with Ken refusing to continue living with Deirdre. He asks her to leave the house.
Each time Ken and Deirdre try to work out their marriage, they have to be cautious not to let Ken's uncle Albert, in whose house they live, and Deirdre's little daughter Tracey know what is at stake. They ask Emily Bishop to see Tracey to school and uncle Albert to have his meals at the 'Rovers Return'. There, people ask Albert why he spends so much time in the pub recently.
Mike Baldwin is also seen in the pub after the incident at the Barlows' house. He reacts in an irritated manner when Ivy Tilsley, who works as supervisor in his factory, comes to ask him some details about a current order at the factory.

---

[6] Hilary Kingsley stresses that Alf Roberts is an Independent councillor in an area where this means Tory and that he is a natural opponent to Ken Barlow who has always displayed left-wing political convictions. (cf. Hilary Kingsley, op.cit., p. 125.).

The Elsie Tanner/Suzie/Marion Storyline
(which is not continued in the subsequent episode)

The two young women, Suzie Birchall who works as barmaid at the 'Rovers Return', and Marion lodge with Elsie Tanner. Suzie's stay is meant to be only temporary. Shortly before she has returned from London in escape from a broken marriage.

Since Suzie, however, used to lodge with Elsie in previous years, she seems to feel that she has the older rights and behaves rather unsociable. Especially, Marion does not get on with her. Suzie is snooty, unreliable and on top of that abuses Marion's boy-friend Eddie Yeats.

This results in a major quarrel. Suzie reacts with her usual callousness and manages that in the end Elsie and Marion are left rowing.

5.2.2.3. *The Stan and Hilda Ogden/Eddie Yeats Storyline*

As so often, the Ogdens have money problems. Stan, who is lazy and obtuse, earns hardly any money as a self-employed window-cleaner and his attempt to get another loan from the local bank is unsuccessful. When Stan tries to buy a beer on credit at the 'Rovers Return', bar-keeper Fred Gee reacts in a very aggressive manner. But Len Fairclough helps out and pays for the beer.

Stan's wife Hilda, who works as a cleaner in several different places, complains that she has to slave for their livelihood.

Eddie Yeats, who lodges with the Ogdens, has a steady job as a binman, presently. Besides, he has just received the good news that his and Marion's building-society account has earned them nearly a hundred Pounds interest.

In view of the Ogdens' pecuniary situation, Eddie decides to give ten Pounds to Stan, who is to give the money to Hilda as supplement to her housekeeping money. But Stan shows not the slightest intention to do so. Rather, as soon as he has got the money, he starts to make his way to the pub, which is, however, prevented by Eddie.

(2nd episode)
On the following day Eddie finds out that Stan wants to spend the money on horse-betting. Now, Eddie sees to it that Hilda gets the money. Hilda defends it resolutely against Stan's attempt to still put it on a horse.

5.2.2.4. *The Bet/Suzie/Fred/Mrs. Walker Storyline*

(1st episode)
Mrs. Walker, the widowed landlady of the 'Rovers Return', is away on holiday at her daughter Joan's. During her absence the staff in the pub, barmaids Bet Lynch and Suzie Birchall and barkeeper Fred Gee, do not take their jobs particularly ser-

ious. Suzie, unreliable as usual, goes to the chemist's during working hours. She is reprimanded by Bet Lynch, but Suzie retorts with her habitual snootiness. Fred Gee attempts to chat Suzie up, asking her in an ambivalent manner to go out with him in his car. But Suzie turns him down without hesitation.

Bet Lynch asks Len Faiclough and Mike Baldwin to confirm "that men really do prefer the svelte mature woman to a young bit of fluff".[7] When Len Fairclough does not agree, she is upset and switches over to another subject, namely the remoteness of the *Street* from everything going on in the rest of the world.

(2nd episode)
On the following day Mrs. Walker returns, her normal pretentious self. Bet Lynch and Hilda Ogden, who also is a charwoman at the 'Rover's Return', are reprimanded for being late. Only Suzie escapes Mrs Walker's reproof, though she came in only a few minutes before the landlady arrived. Bet reproaches Suzie with fawning upon Mrs. Walker.

Fred complains that Mrs. Walker takes advantage of him, ordering him about and not even refunding the petrol money when he picked her up at the station. Bet in a rather derisive and offensive manner tells him that he is a coward.[8] Later in the day Bet persuades Fred to claim his money back from Mrs. Walker. But Mrs. Walker shrewdly evades Fred's nudge, pointing to the "cold wind that is blowing through the licence trade".[9] Before and after that incident, Fred is derided by some of the women customers in the pub. In addition, Suzie turns down another invitation by him.

5.2.3.   Characters

5.2.3.1.   *The Characters Featured in The Two Episodes*
(in chronological order according to their appearance in the two episodes):

1.)   Eddie Yeats--a binman /lodges with the Ogdens.
2.)   Chalkie, his colleague who is not a resident of Coronation Street.
3.)   Elsie Tanner
4.)   Suzie Birchall, barmaid/lodges with Elsie Tanner.
5.)   Marion--Eddie Yeats' girlfriend/also lodges with Elsie Tanner.
6.)   Deirdre Barlow, shop-assistant.
7.)   Ken Barlow, unemployed at the moment.
8.)   Emily Bishop, Mike Baldwin's secretary and Deirdre's motherly friend.

---

[7]   Shooting transcript episode one, sequence 6, scene 2, shot 2.

[8]   cf. shooting transcript episode two, sequence 4, scene 3, shot 3.

[9]   episode two, sequence 9, scene 1 (this scene is not included in the shooting transcript in the appendix)

9.) Alf Roberts, owner of the corner-shop and local councillor.
10.) Mike Baldwin, factory owner.
11.) Stan and Hilda Ogden, window-cleaner and charwoman.
12.) Tracey Langton, Deirdre's little daughter from her first husband.
13.) Bet Lynch, barmaid.
14.) Fred Gee, barkeeper.
15.) Len Fairclough--owner of a small building-yard (he is married to Rita).
16.) Mr. Colfax, bank-manager/he is not a resident of Coronation Street.
17.) Albert Tatlock, Ken's old uncle/he lives with Ken and Deirdre in the house which he owns
18.) Ivy Tilsley, supervisor at Mike Baldwin's factory (then married to Bert Tilsley).
19.) Vera Duckworth, another Baldwin employee (married to Jack Duckworth).

5.2.3.2. The Curricula Vitae of The Key Characters of The Two Episodes

Deirdre Barlow:

Deirdre Barlow, née Hunt has been a resident of Coronation Street since 1973. Her mother, Blanche Hunt managed the corner-shop for some time. In 1973 she started to work as a secretary in Len Faiclough's building-yard, in the two episodes under consideration she is working as shop assistant in the corner-shop. After breaking off her engagement with Annie Walker's son Billy, she married Ray Langton in 1975, with whom she had a daughter, Tracey. Ray left her in 1980. In 1981 she got married to Ken Barlow, after having decided between him and Mike Baldwin. Ken, Deirdre and her daughter. Tracey live at No. 1, Coronation Street with Ken's Uncle Albert.

Deirdre is in her late twenties, wears spectacles and has never been particularly good-looking. But now, in contrast to a few years ago, she looks rather gaunt and dowdy.[10] The clothes she wears in the two episodes are analysed as ordinary and almost tasteless. It is noticeable that her skirt in the two episodes is made out of the same cloth as her little daughter Tracey's dress, which suggests that she is an efficient house-wife. She has a strong Manchester accent which indicates that educationally she is inferior to Ken.

"Deirdre is customarily hot-tempered and resilient."[11] But over the years due to various turns of fate she has become more vulnerable and at times displays a certain whining waywardness. In the two episodes under consideration she is suggested as a woman who acts impulsively and grabs what she can[12] in fear of being

---

[10] The actress Anne Kirkbride had anorexia, which at that time left her quite thin.

[11] Marion Jordan, Character Types and The Individual, op. cit., p. 74.

[12] cf. shooting transcript episode one, sequence 11, scene I, shot 8.

missed out by life.[13]

In subsequent episodes the Deirdre/Mike affair will be terminated by Deirdre's decision to continue living with Ken.

But three years later, in 1986 old wounds left over from that affair are reopened when Mike Baldwin starts a relationship with Susan, Ken's daughter from his first marriage.

In 1987 Ken affecs that Deirdre (since he himself cannot do so without risking his job) stands for and wins the election as local councillor against Alf Roberts. Deirdre starts to like her new job. The amount of time she has to spend on it, however, causes new tension between her and Ken. In 1990 it comes to a new culmination in the Ken/Deirdre marriage relation which results in Ken leaving his wife for another woman. Deirdre, however, reacts more relieved than angry, grasping Ken's absence as an increase in her personal freedom.

Ken Barlow:

Ken is the scholarship boy of the early episodes and at the time of the two episodes is in his early forties. He has had a rather unsettled career, working variously as personnel officer, teacher, writer warehouse executive, taxi-driver, and as Community Welfare Officer in the Community Centre in Coronation Street. (Subsequently, he will become editor of the *local* newspaper the *Weatherfield Recorder*.)

In the episodes in question he is unemployed. The marriage with Deirdre is his third marriage. In 1962 he got married to his first wife, Valerie Tatlock (uncle Albert's niece), a hairdresser with whom he had twins. Valerie died in 1971 electrocuted by a defect hairdryer. His twins were eventually taken to Glasgow to be cared for by Valerie's mother. In 1973 Ken got married a second time, to Janet Reid. But the marriage did not last for very long. They soon separated.[14] In 1977 Janet committed suicide through a drug overdose. In 1981 Ken got married to Deirdre Langton, née Hunt.

Ken has also had affairs with several other women "both between and during his marriage".[15]

Politically he has always been more inclined to the left. During his university years he was active in the ban-the-bomb movement and later participated in anti-Vietnam-War demonstrations. Despite that, mainly due to his higher education, he is portrayed as an eminently respectable figure; sometimes he appears pompous. His accent is much more standard than the accents of most of the other characters. It belongs to Ken's image of respectability that he is frequently seen in a

---

[13] cf. shooting transcript episode one, sequence 13, scene 1, shot 23.

[14] Ken does not mention that second marriage but only refers to his first marriage in the second episode (shooting transcript episode two, sequence 6, scene 3) under consideration.

[15] Marion Jordan, Character..., p. 75.

Ken Barlow in 1990 looking for a job once again

Photo: Granada Television

Mike Baldwin in 1991 with two of the women he lived with more recently, long after his affair with Deirdre Barlow

Photo: Granada Television

suit. Over the years he has become corpulent. In the two episodes under consideration, he displays an air of frustration. In his role as a cuckolded husband he seems more moralistic than angry. The assault on Deirdre appears rather like an act against his usual serial type.

As the affair is eventually terminated in his favour, he can claim a victory over Baldwin, whom he detests, only to be humiliated three years later when Baldwin marries his 23-year-old daughter Susan. That marriage, however, destined to fail ends in Susan leaving her much older husband and aborting their child.

Already in the two episodes under consideration, Ken concedes an attitude towards Deirdre which suggests him as a male chauvinist. This feature is further emphasized in subsequent years when Ken reproaches Deirdre with neglecting her family over her work as a local councillor, though the main reason why she stood for election had been Ken's own political ambition. In 1990 Ken leaves Deirdre to live with another woman.

Albert Tatlock

Albert Tatlock in whose house the Barlows live, is the uncle of Ken's first wife Valerie. He has been the grumpy grandfather figure since the serial first started and, together with Ena Sharples, Minnie Caldwell and Martha Longhurst, formed the 'gang' of four senior citizens who used to meet in the snug of the 'Rover's Return'. Albert whose favourite drink is rum sternly sticks to his memories as a soldier in the first World War and his grudge against the 'Jerries'.
He will die in the following year 1984.

Mike Baldwin:

"He entered Coronation Street in 1976 when he bought the then disused Warehouse and converted it into his second factory (...)".[16] With his Cockney accent he is the only regular character from the South of England.
At the time of the two episodes, he is an energetic businessman in his early forties, a self-made man and, as he considers himself, a "lady's man".[17] Kingsley writes: "Baldwin (...) has a second-hand Jaguar and a cheap line in smalltalk that usually ensnares gullible females into corny candle-lit dinners for two with soft music and low light."[18]

Baldwin who is divorced from his first wife who lives in London, has had relationships with several women in the *Street*, eg. Bet Lynch, Suzie Birchall and also with Deirdre before she got married to Ken.

---

[16] Marion Jordan, Character Type and the Individual, op. cit., p. 74.

[17] Richard Paterson and John Stewart, Street Life. In: Richard Dyer et al, p. 85.

[18] Hilary Kingsley, op. cit., p. 91.

Baldwin is not actually a rogue though he knows his tricks. In the context of the two episodes he is not portrayed as an unscrupulous malefactor but rather as somebody who naturally makes use of the opportunities given to him.

In 1986 Baldwin reenactes the confrontation with Ken Barlow over a woman when at the age of 44 he starts courting Ken's young daughter Susan.

Stan and Hilda Ogden

Stan and Hilda Ogden are the couple whose marriage between 1963 and 1984 was portrayed as the most permanent of all the relationships in *Coronation Street*. It only ended when fat and lazy Stan died of a heart attack in 1984. Hilda stayed in *Coronation Street* for another three years before she moved away to be the housekeeper of Dr. Lowther.

Stan and Hilda Ogden were major warrants of *Coronation Street's* comical qualities, though after Stan's death Hilda apparently could not fulfill that part on her own. Hilary Kingsley suggests: "(...) she changed from being the comic-relief sharp-tongued nosy char into the best-loved woman on television."[19]

However, in the two episodes analysed the conventional interaction of the weighty, lethargic and workshy window cleaner Stan and his lean, strident, constantly nagging wife Hilda, who was rarely seen without mac und curlers, is still intact.
Stan has never been very inclined to earn money by hard work. Instead, he is prone to spend the little money he makes on beer. Due to Stan's laziness and deteriorating health, it is Hilda who through several cleaning jobs puts "the fish and chips on the table for 'tea' and pays the bills for the humblest house in Coronation Street, number 13"[20].
In the two episodes analysed, as throughout her entire serial existence, Hilda displays a stoical sense of survival. Much of the comedy is brought about by her lack of education and her ridiculed attempts of sophistication.

Eddie Yeats

Eddie Yeats who in the two episodes analysed lodges with the Ogdens and works as a binman, is an ex-burglar with several prison sentences on his records. He arrived in Coronation Street in 1974 after his dismissal from gaol and in 1983 he seems to be reformed with a steady job and a girl-friend. But in between 1974 and 1983, while living in Coronation Street, he committed another burglary and was put to prison. Kingsley describes him as "looking like a badly made suet pud-

---

[19] ibid., p. 119.

[20] ibid.

ding, with a silly laugh and a daft gap-toothed grin"[21].

Despite that, he is loved by his fiancée Marion to whom he will get married in the subsequent time and with whom he will move away from Coronation Street to live in Bury.

Elsie Tanner

Elsie Tanner is the sexy, sharp-tongued slut and abandonned mother of two grown-up children of the first episode. Throughout the 23 years of her serial existence (interrupted by her absence from *Coronation Street* in the seventies) she worked in various low-profile jobs to make ends meet but had four husbands and numerous lovers. Kingsley characterizes her as "the sexiest woman (...), easily conned, susceptible to flattery, emotional, and quick to fall in love"[22]. Soon after the two episodes, still in the year 1983, she will leave Coronation Street to follow an old flame to Portugal.

Suzie Birchall

Suzie moved into Coronation Street as Elsie's lodger and 'foster' daughter in 1978. Like Elsie in her younger years, she had a turbulent love-life.
Some time before the two episodes, she left for London. But at the time of the Ken/Deirdre/Mike crisis she has just returned in escape from a broken marriage.
In one of the following episodes she will be beaten up by her husband Terry who follows her North. Later in the year 1983 she will again disappear from Weatherfield.

Bet Lynch

Bet Lynch entered Coronation Street as a regular in 1970 when she became the new barmaid of the 'Rover's Return'. In 1974 it became known that she had an illegitimate son who at that time had been killed in a car crash while serving with the Army in Northern Ireland. Bet had numerous unlucky love-affairs, which also included Coronation Street residents Len Fairclough, Mike Baldwin and her boss Billy Walker. In 1983 Bet is still Coronation Street's "failed tart" who hides her desperation by over-dressing.[23]

---

[21] ibid., p. 146.

[22] ibid., pp. 132/133.

[23] ibid., p. 115.

But in 1985 when the Walkers give up the tenacy of the 'Rover's Return', Bet becomes the landlady of the pub. In 1987 she has run into debts, the main reason why she consented to marry Alec Gilroy, to whom she owes the money. Subsequently, Bet's outward appearance changes. According to Kingsley, "the polyester cocktail collection, the earings which ranged from parakeets swinging on perches to miniature lavatory-bowls, were giving way to smart stripped blouses, plain skirts and tasteful costume necklaces".[24]

Annie Walker

Annie Walker was already the landlady of the 'Rover's Return' when *Coronation Street* first started and still is in 1983 at the time of the two episodes. She has managed the pub on her own from 1970 when her husband Jack died. Annie, despite coming from a well concealed humble family background, has always considered herself morally aloof and more refined and sophisticated than most of the other denizens of Coronation Street. Thus, she objected to her son Billy's decision to employ Bet Lynch on the grounds that she was too common.

Later in the year 1983 Annie Walker will retire from Coronation Street to live with her daughter Joan. For the following two years the tenancy of the pub will be held by her son Billy, whose 'moral lapses' Annie Walker always bore with a great amount of patience and self-restraint.

---

[24] ibid., p. 116.

5.3. The Form of The Two Episodes

5.3.1. The Outer Structure

The following list displays the number of sequences per episode, the number of shots, characters involved and partially also the setting. Episode two, however, has not been fully transcribed; the opening and closing sequences, the commercials and most of sequences two, four, seven and nine have been left out. That is why of these sequences only the duration and settings are listed.

Episode one

Sequ.	Dur./min./sec.	Character/setting	No. of shots
0	0/19	Opening sequence	6
1	1/23	Elsie Tanner/Marion/Suzie/Eddie	15
2	1/52	Deirdre/Ken	24
3	1/25	(shop) Ken/Alf/Mike	17
4	2/19	Stan/Hilda/Eddie	13
5	1/35	Ken/Deirdre	5
6	1/57	(Rovers Return) Bet/Fred/Suzie/Len/Mike	18
7	1/22	(outside on the street) Stan/bank manager	13
Commercials	2/35		
8	0/58	(shop) Alf/Deirdre/Mike	6
9	1/47	(Rovers Return) Stan/Eddie/Len/Fred/Suzie	15
10	1/48	Stan/Hilda/Eddie Yeats	3
11	2/01	(shop) Deirdre/Emily/Alf	12
12	1/50	Elsie Tanner/Suzie/Marion	10
13	4/01	Ken/Deirdre	32
14	0/59	closing sequence	1

Episode two

Sequ.	Dur./min./sec.	Character/setting	No. of shots
1	1/15	Ken/uncle Albert	13
2	2/45	Stan/Hilda/Eddie/Mike Baldwin	incomplete
3	2/33	Ken/Deirdre/uncle Albert/Tracey/ Emily Bishop	15
4	2/53	(Rover's Return) Hilda/Suzie/ Bet/Fred/Mrs. Walker	incomplete
5	0/51	Ken/Deirdre	4
Commercials			
6	3/44	Ken/Deirdre/Albert	4
7	0/57	(Baldwin's office)	incomplete
8	2/31	Ken/Deirdre/Mike	8
9	2/50	(Rover's Return)	incomplete
10	2/54	Ken/Deirdre/Tracey	22

As the diagram shows, episode one has 13 different sequences. Each sequence is set in a different location, either in one of the houses, the pub or the shop; all together there are six locations alternating in the thirteen sequences.

Three sequences are set in Ken and Deirdre Barlow's and uncle Albert's house and a further three are set in the corner shop where Deirdre works as shop assistant. Two sequences are set inside of Stan and Hilda Ogden's house. A further two sequences are set outside and inside of Elsie Tanner's house. The 'Rover's Return' is the site of two sequences and another sequence is set in the street in front of the local branch of a bank.

It is obvious that already in episode one more scope is given to the Deirdre/Ken storyline than to any of the other storylines. Thus, sequence 13, for instance, in which Deirdre tells Ken about the affair with Baldwin, is much longer than the other sequences and has 32 shots. Sequence two, which also features Ken and Deirdre, has 24 shots. None of the other sequences has more than 18 shots.

Episode two, however, consists merely of ten sequences and switches between only four locations. Six of the ten sequences are set in Ken and Deirdre Barlow's and Albert Tatlock's house, one is set in Mike Baldwin's office.

This reflects that the second episode is even more dominated by the Ken/Deirdre/Mike storyline than the preceding episode. In contrast to episode one, the shots in the sequences which feature Ken and Deirdre in episode two last much longer. As mentioned before, sequence 13 of episode one (4 min. 1 sec.) has 32 shots. Whereas sequence 6 of episode two (3 min. 44 sec.) has only four shots. The only sequence of episode two with a fast-paced succession of shots comparable to sequences featuring the two characters in episode one, is sequence 10 with 22 shots (within two min. 54 sec.).

Thus in episode two the emphasis is clearly put on the lengthy dialogues between Ken and Deirdre. These are considered interesting and exciting enough for the viewer without the dramatic thickening which quick shot/shot reverse successions evoke.

Only sequence ten of episode two is marked by a faster succession of shot. This is a device to heighten the dramatic tension towards the end of the episode and for the build-up towards the final cliffhanger, namely Ken's demand that Deirdre must move out.

As suggested before, episodes of *Coronation Street* are normally successions of linear narrative syntagms, that is to say sequences in Christian Metz' terminology. In some cases these sequences can be subdivided into scenes, as is reflected in the shooting transcript.

The two episodes under consideration are no exceptions in that respect. Only in episode two, sequence eight, shot three is this convention broken. Sequence eight is set in the Barlows' house. Deirdre receives a telephone call from Mike Baldwin. But they are interrupted by Ken who snatches the receiver away from Deirdre and puts it down again. The next shot shows Baldwin in his office taking his coat to leave. The following shot shows Ken and Deirdre again in their house.

The linearity of sequence eight is broken by the insertion of the 'Baldwin shot'.

This device heightens the dramatic tension in that sequence, which culminates in Baldwin's arrival at the Barlows' house and Ken's assault on Deirdre.

5.3.2. The Use of Time in the Two Episodes

Elsewhere it has been suggested that *Coronation Street*, like other continuous serials, evokes the impression to portray a parallel life, with the fictional time largely corresponding with time in real life. In the episodes under consideration, remarks made by the characters insinuate that the episodes are set in February.[25]

But as is always the case in the portrayal of extraordinary events in the serial, only one night has passed between the end of episode one and the beginning of episode two[26], whereas in reality the episode was shown several days later than episode one. That is why the fictional time in episode two cannot correspond with the actual day of the week.

The narrated time of each episode encompasses one entire day. Both episodes start in the morning and end in the early evening, in both episodes it is approximately lunch-time when the narrative is interrupted by the break for the commercials.

While the individual sequences are chronological and linear, the fictional time elapses in between the different sequences.

5.3.3. The Narrative Structure and Its Implications

The narrative structure of *Coronation Street* is closely linked to the spacial arrangements and the particular sense of community in the Street. Thus, most storylines change with the setting and are joined together in various communal meeting places, especially the pub and the corner shop.

In the first episode the sequences which belong to the Ken/Deirdre storyline are either set in their home or in the corner shop where Deirdre works. They alternate with sequences featuring Elsie Tanner and her lodgers, the Ogdens and Eddie Yeats, or people in the pub.

In the second episode analysed the Ken/Deirdre/Mike sequences alternate with sequences showing the Ogdens or people in the pub.

Marion Jordan stresses that in *Coronation Street* public and private life are closely interrelated, which means that people rarely seclude themselves from the rest of the community. This, according to her, happens only in times of crisis.[27] In the second episode analysed the narrative follows exactly that pattern. Deirdre and Ken, in the midst of their marriage crisis, withdraw to their private domestic

---

[25] cf. shooting transcript episode one, sequence 6, scene 2, shot 8.

[26] ibid. p. 26 episode one, sequence 2, scene 1, shot 3.

[27] cf. Marion Jordan, Realism and Convention. In: Richard Dyer et al., op. cit., p. 30.

sphere. Deirdre does neither go out to work nor take Tracey to school and uncle Albert is sent to the pub for his meals.

In the two episodes under consideration, the knowledge of the affair has been not yet spread out. Only Emily Bishop and the people directly involved (and the viewer) know about it. It is part of the dramatic tension of the episodes that the viewer can expect that it seeps through to the rest of the community at any time. Already uncle Albert's frequent appearance in the pub and Baldwin's irritated re-action in episode two, (sequence nine, scene three, shot one), are likely to arouse the suspicion of the others.

Yet, the revelation of what is at stake is postponed until the next episode.

The question of *how* the affair will be revealed, first to Ken and eventually to the rest of the community, is a major source of tension.

As has been explained elsewhere, the different storylines in *Coronation Street* are not only linked in an explicit linear way, through gossip in one of the communal meeting places or through one character's involvement in several storylines, but also in a more implicit manner on an associative level.

Thus, in the first episode a line of associations is built up which centres upon the topic of work. Ken has not been accepted for the job for which he applied. With the Ogdens, work is also a topic, as Stan has been loafing again and Hilda has to work for their livelihood. Stan's laziness somehow is a parody of Ken's alleged lack of vigour, Hilda's nagging a reflection upon Deirdre's complaint that Ken ist not energetic enough.

With Suzie Birchall work also becomes a topic, Suzie not only avoids doing her share of the housework at Elsie Tanner's but also does not do her job at the pub properly during Mrs. Walker's absence.

A more positive attitude to work is put forward through the person of Eddie Yeats. In the two episodes Eddie seems to be suggested as the 'shining example' of a positive work ethics. The very first scene of the first episode analysed, depicts him on his early-morning round as a binman. A later scene in which he shows the letter from the building society to Hilda, suggests that he is also thrifty. Nevertheless, he is generous enough to give ten Pounds to Stan and Hilda in an act of solidarity.

A second line of associations in the first episode reflects upon the nature of women. At the end of this episode it is to be revealed that Deirdre has for several weeks concealed an affair from her husband. This event and the subsequent quarrel are foreshadowed in the other storylines, by Hilda's nagging, Bet Lynch's remark about "the svelte mature woman"[28], by Suzie Birchall's bitchy treatment of Fred, by Marion's proclamation that "she is not a woman for nought"[29] and by the quarrel between Bet Lynch and Suzie, and by the row between Elsie, Marion and Suzie in the sequence immediately before the sequence, in which Deirdre's affair

---

[28] Shooting transcript, episode one, sequence 6, scene 2, shot 2.

[29] ibid., episode one, sequence 6, scene 2, shot 5.

is revealed to Ken.

A similar attempt seems to be made to reflect on the nature of men, though the line of associations is not as strong as with the women.

The Stan/Ken analogy seems to suggest that men lack energy. Bet Lynch's teasing question to Len Fairclough of which type of women men do prefer and Suzie's speculation on why Eddie comes to their house in the morning alludes to men's sexual preferences.

The narrative structure of the second episode analysed is clearly dominated by the storyline which centres upon Ken's and Deirdre's marital relationship. This storyline, however, is reflected upon and parodied on various levels in the other storylines. Thus, the stories about the Ogdens are used as a humorous reflection of the Barlow marriage theme.

At the time when the two episodes were broadcast it had become a convention of the programme that stories about broken marriages were counterbalanced by stories dealing with the Ogdens, whose marriage used to be portrayed as extraordinary permanent. However, that permanency was almost invariably presented in a funny way . In that the episodes under consideration are no exceptions. The following exclamation by Hilda speaks for itself:

> "Don't talk to me about handicaps! I've been livin' with one for the last thirty odd year."[30]

More 'comic relief' in the serious atmosphere of the second episode is brought about by the cantankerous and stingy character of uncle Albert. Albert who lives with the Barlows (or rather the Barlows live in his house) does not hide that he is more attached to Deirdre than to his nephew (though without knowing anything about the affair).[31]

Incidentally, the 'uncle-Albert sub-storyline' introduces another minor theme: the relation between the young and the old generation. In the pen-ultimate sequence of the last episode, Albert stresses that the house in which the Barlows and he live belongs to him, by pointing out:

> "Look, if there's any chuckin'-out to be done, it'll be me who does it!"[32]

On one hand this foreshadows the climax of the following sequence in which Ken demands that Deirdre moves out, but on the other hand it already takes away the sting from that demand, since it is uncle Albert who does "the chucking-out".

It is another conspicuous feature of the narrative structure of the second episode that the more Deirdre's initially strong position in the marital dispute is

---

[30] ibid., episode two, sequence 2, scene 2, shot 6.

[31] ibid., episode two, sequence one, scene 1, shot 6.

[32] Shooting transcript, episode two, sequence 9, scene 2, shot 2.

undermined, the more the image of female strength is stressed in other storylines. This is, for instance, reflected in Hilda's and Mrs. Walker's bossy behaviour towards men or in the derision with which factory women Ivy Tilsley and Vera Duckworth treat Fred Gee. Bet Lynch also treats Fred in a very offensive manner when she says to him:

> "Nearly quite cheeky then weren't you. I had a cat once, a Tom... only short for a couple of things. Puts me amind of you, love."[33]

5.3.4. The Visual Style of The Two Episodes

The overall visual style of the two episodes analysed does not deviate from the then still usual naturalism of the serial. The outside scenes are obviously shot on a bleak and rainy day and there is nothing glamorous in the first scene of episode two, set in a dreary back-lane. The inside scenes also portray quite naturalistically the appurtenances of the small sets.

The camera style is marked by the conventional use of mainly eye-level shots, varying only between close-up and medium with occasional full shots and one long shot (in episode one, sequence 7, scene 1, shot 13).
Only in some scenes of episode two there are deviations from the normal camera style, due to the fact that the marriage crisis constitutes an extraordinary event.
Already in episode one there are some visual hints to the extraordinary character of these episodes, reflected, for instance, in the detail shot of Ken's hands cutting bread in sequence two, scene 1, shot 1. In episode two, sequence 7, shot 8 there is another detail shot, this time depicting Baldwin's hand dialing a telephone number. At this point the detail shot clearly contributes to the dramatic tension of that part of episode two, shortly before Baldwin arrives at the Barlow's house.
A further deviation from the conventional camera style, which occurs only in episode two is the use of high - and in one case also low - camera angles. The low angle shot is in episode two, sequence 2, scene 1, shot 1, depicting Baldwin's approaching car. This shot likewise engenders a certain dramatic tension, as if suggesting 'here he comes soon there will be trouble'.
Extraordinary high camera angles are used in some of the scenes in episode two in which the Barlows are depicted. Examples are in sequence 1, scene 1, shot 1, or in sequence 3, scene 1, shot 1. In these two cases the high camera angles seem to engender an atmosphere of uneasiness and melancholic tension. A high camera angle is also used in sequence eight, scene 1, shot 2 of episode two, in which Deirdre is shown receiving the telephone call from Baldwin. At this point the high angle shot has the effect of heightening the dramatic tension even more; a few shots further Ken assaults Deirdre.
The shot following the assault which depicts Ken with his shirt torn open, is also marked by a high camera angle. Albeit the high angle shot at that point seems to

---

[33] ibid., episode two, sequence 4, scene 3, shot 3.

have less the effect of arousing tension. Rather it evokes a certain distancing effect, as if suggesting that Ken's action cannot be approved of or that it contradicts his normal character.

The camera style in episode two seems to fulfill part of the function which in other film - and television narratives is fulfilled by music, namely the creation of atmosphere. But, since camera movements, even in the lengthy shots of episode two, are relatively scarce and slow, the allegedly highly dramatic events of that episode appear wooden.

5.4. The Representation of Class and Gender in The Two Episodes

5.4.1. Gender

The investigation of the narrative structure reveals that the gender opposition, which reaches a climax in the Ken/Deirdre dispute, is an important underlying pattern of the two episodes.
Thus, several storylines, particularly in the first episode, seem to reflect upon the nature of women and men.
Although men are not explicitly portrayed as weak, the overall image which especially the first episode conveys, is one of female strength. But this image is mainly built on rather ambivalent stereotypical female characteristics: women are bitchy, bossy, nagging, demanding, aggressive and quarrelsome with eachother.

As suggested elsewhere, the programme up to then did not question the traditional female roles of housewife and mother, though it is a convention of the serial that most women have a job outside the house. Thus, in the first episode analysed Ken suggests to Deirdre, that her life is rounded because she has got a family, a home, a job and friends" [34].
Deirdre's reaction is "that she does not want a boring life"[35]. But her aspirations to a more exciting life are mainly linked to Ken's showing more vigour to get a better job, which implicitly stresses the traditional male role.
Hilda's complaint that her mother never put in the hours she does nor her grandmother[36], on one hand suggests a certain sense of matrilinial relationships but at the same time it stresses that the main breadwinner ought to be the husband and that she unfortunately has to put up with a deviation from that norm.

The Ken/Deirdre marriage crisis is worked through without great psychological depth in plain common-sense terms, with a few rather frank allusions to sex.

---

[34] Shooting transcript., episode one, sequence 13, scene 1.

[35] ibid.

[36] ibid., episode one, sequence 10, scene 1.

The reasons why Deirdre started an affair with Baldwin, according to her, are that "she needed someone to turn to"[37] because Ken does not really listen to her and she wanted something Ken "wouldn't give her"[38].
The latter remark is given a sexual connotation by Ken who says "I know what you wanted."[39]

It is noticeable that on an explicit level, Deirdre's initially strong position is gradually undermined by Ken's interpreting the affair from his point of view. That point of view largely reflects a dominant moral code: "if you want to stay married, you don't give in to it."[40]
According to Ken's moral standards Deirdre must move out.

But as indicated before, the explicit predominance of Ken's position and the moral code it represents is rendered doubtful by the vein of assertive femininity which runs through the other storylines of the second episode. Besides, it is rendered questionable in the light of the narrative rules of the continuous serial, which are determined by the constant need for new storylines that defies marital relationships which are too permanent. The impact of that generic requirement is also reflected in Deirdre's and Ken's 'curricula vitae'.

5.4.2. Class

The overall set up of the programme with its solidified image of being about working-class culture affects that most stories have at least a tentative reference to class.
Richard Paterson and John Stuart suggest with regard to the strike episodes mentioned with before that "the gender opposition is mapped on a class opposition".
The opposite seems to be true in the episodes analysed; here class oppositions are apparently mapped on the gender opposition.

The Ken/Deirdre conflict also has a dimension of social class. Deirdre's broad accent, which in the frame of reference of the programme is perhaps the most important emblem of a working-class background, suggests her as educational inferior to her husband Ken, who through higher education has outgrown the working class.
Deirdre claims that the usual style of Ken's conversation with her resembles "a missionary talking to the natives".[41]

---

[37] ibid., episode two, sequence 2, scene 3.

[38] ibid., episode two, sequence 10, scene 1.

[39] ibid.

[40] ibid.

[41] Shooting transcript, episode two, sequence 6, scene 3.

Another incident in the programme, which could be interpreted as a reference to class is Bet Lynch's remark on people who go skiing "all white teeths and tans, lookin' like great admirals",[42] with whom people in *Coronation Street* have no connection.

In both cases, however, it is a very blurred concept of class which shines through. With Deirdre, class is represented merely by educational standards. Whereas in the incident with Bet Lynch it is really primarily the inside/outside opposition, inherent to the narrative structure of the serial, which is (perhaps ironically) reflected upon.
Consequently, the conclusion from the strike episodes, namely that the programme has a tendency to mitigate the class conflict by projecting it on other types of conflict, is also confirmed by the present analysis.

More explicit references to class are contained in the Ogden-storyline of the first episode. There Hilda Ogden infers:

"Oh, it's right what they say, ya know, more makes more. That's why folks like us never 'ave a chance, 'cause we start with nothin' and twice nothin' is still only nothin'. Idn't it?"[43]

Social critical though this remark appears, from the mouth of Hilda Ogden, who within the frame of reference of the serial was established as a funny character and an outsider, it acquires a comic connotation. Besides, the feckless lifestyle of the Ogdens suggests that it is their own fault. Hilda also says: "Mind you, not that some of it is not our own fault".[44] The fact that the Ogdens are apparently not even familiar with the possibility of saving money in a building society account and that Stan obviously is not even properly insured (he has not heard of BUPA)[45], suggests them as simple-minded and careless.

The political dimension of labour relations are blurred by Hilda's cynical common-sense remark on trade unions. "And what are the Unions after, ha? 35 hour week, I do a 35 hour day. What 'ave I got to show for it?"[46]

Within the frame of reference of the two episodes the character of Eddie Yeats seems to be suggested as a counter-image to the Ogdens. Eddie appears to be imbued with a certain middle-class work ethic.

But similar to the moral codes applied in the Deirdre/Ken storyline, the long-term structure of the programme undermines the explicit exposition of the

---

[42] ibid., episode one, sequence 6, scene 2.

[43] ibid., episode one, sequence 4, scene 2.

[44] ibid.

[45] Shooting transcript, episode one, sequence 7, scene 1.

[46] ibid., episode one, sequence 10, scene 1.

Ogdens' failure in finding the morsels which an achievement-oriented, capitalist society strews out for them. For, long-term viewers know Eddie Yeats, who is suggested as a 'shining example' (a paradox in itself in connection with a binman) of work discipline and thrift, as a loafer and n'ver-do-well of earlier episodes, which renders the comparison between him and the Ogdens ambivalent.

The ambivalence in both cases can be attributed to the narrative excess of soap opera, emphasized by Robert Allen.[47]

---

[47] cf. Chapter one, p. 7

6.   CONCLUSION

The narrative form of the continuous television serial or soap opera, on which *Coronation Street* is based, constitutes one of several different types of serialized fiction conveyed by the television medium. Incidentally, the serial form has been a characteristic of popular fiction and drama for many centuries. However, the technical innovations of the 19th century added a new industrial and highly commercial element, which ever since has influenced the production of popular fiction serials in the print - and electronic media. It is within that historical context that the soap opera which is marked by a streamlined mode of production, can be suggested as a system of cultural production that closely reverberates the main mode of production in an industrialized society.

Yet, a long-standing continuous serial with its infinite narrative structure can never be described as a finite product. Rather, it is, due to the constant need for new storylines and the competition with other serials, influenced by changing audience preferences and also by more general cultural and social trends.

As far as *Coronation Street* is concerned, it constitutes the prototype of the Social Realist early-prime-time soap opera. Other more recent serials in Britain, such as *Brookside* (Channel Four) and *EastEnders* (BBC1), also followed that type of serial. The competition with those newer serials, but more implicitly also with more glamorous soap operas such as *Dallas*, *Dynasty* and *Neighbours* imported from America and Australia, has brought about major changes in the thirty-year-old *Coronation Street* at the end of the Eighties. That is not to say though that before *Coronation Street* was not subject to gradual change. For, changes have always occured in the serial through long-standing characters'leaving and new ones joining and in reflection of more general changes in British life. However, such reflections appeared almost invariably retarded, mediated by the inherent nostalgia of the serial and a set of conventions rooted in the cultural climate of the late fifties and early sixties.

The recent changes in the texture of the serial affected a decrease in its customary visual naturalism through the use of more colour and light and a moderate increase in glamour reflected in the outward appearances of most characters and their homes. This can be interpreted both, as a silent concession in the generic competition with the more glamorous American and Australian soap operas and also as a reflection of the more general spirit of aspiration that marked the latter half of the Thatcher era in Britain. A symbol of the business ideals of that era could be seen in the super-market, which since 1989 has supplemented the smaller shops which have been part of the *Coronation Street* setting ever since it started.

Yet, such symbols and images seem to be limited and subverted by comical devices and the endlessness of the serial narrative. Thus, Curly Watts, the slightly

weird trainee manager of the super-market is only a caricature Yuppy whom long-term viewers remember as scrap dealer of some years before.
In a 1990 sequence of episodes customary comical hints to the conventional old-fashioned character of the serial justify that the Rover's Return is finally saved from being converted into a trendy American-style theme pub.

Before, the serial relied mainly on a core of middle-aged and some quite old characters. Whereas the emphasis now - as a decade before in some of the long-standing American daytime serials - has shifted more towards younger characters. Likewise, the serial seems to be more open to feature racial minorities, though the regular appearance of non-white characters is still kept at a relative low level if compared, for instance, to *EastEnders*. Expressed in Robert Allen's term, *Coronation Street* more than other British serials, seems to be marked by the 'paradigmatic dilemma' which the full incorporation of characters from ethnic minorities into the long-term relational structure of soap opera causes in a society with racial prejudices.[1]

Following an overall trend in the soap opera genre, which has also been reflected in the two above-mentioned more recent British soap operas, *Coronation Street* since about 1989 has featured more crime and violence.

Another more general development in the soap opera genre in America and Britain has likewise affected *Coronation Street*. Namely an increase in the - for budgetary reasons - traditionally few scenes set outside the studio precinct. In *Coronation Street* such scenes are usually shot in the Manchester area. But on a few occasions characters could - similar to their counterparts in other British soaps - also be followed on trips outside Manchester, some even to foreign countries. According to producer Mervyn Watson, "the world of the inhabitants of Coronation Street has geographically expanded".

Due to the changes described and the increased screen presence of the serial through a third weekly episode, it could in 1989 regain its position as one of the most popular programmes and in many weeks *the* most popular programme in Britain, while its main rival since 1986, the BBC1 serial *EastEnders*, has presently fallen behind.
The relative stability which has marked the popularity rates of the Granada serial, seems to suggest that it can also survive the current shake-up of the commercial television sector in Britain, which has been affected by the implementation of the 1990 Broadcasting Act. Even if, likely or not, Granada did not regain the north-western franchise, this is unlikely to kill *Coronation Street*. For, Granada could still continue producing the serial as an independent contractor of the new franchise holder, who probably would not want to do without such a stable warrant of large audiences.

---

[1] cf. p.7 of this book.

However, in the long run *Coronation Street* is likely to be affected by a more relaxed code of advertising and sponsorship under the new legislation. This could - like it has traditionally been the case with the North and South American continuous serials - also imply that advertisers were allowed to advertise via product placement in the serial and not just through the insertion of commercials, clearly distinguishable from the narrative.

Within the still tentative concept of an international genre of the continuous serial or soap opera proposed in this book (drawing on Lévi-Strauss' concept of myth, which describes the same or similar basic structures operating in different cultures and social contexts), *Coronation Street* would constitute a distinct British variation of the US-American continuous serial. The US-American or Anglo/American continuous serial deviates in a number of narrative and stylistic aspects from the Latin American type of continuous serial.

In comparison with past and present continuous long-running serials in the United States where the form was first developed because of advertising interests, *Coronation Street* distinguishes itself mainly through its Social Realist and comic features.
The Social Realism of the programme has been brought about in variation of the traditional Soap Opera Realism. Basic narrative features of the soap opera form are its focus on a group of characters instead of just one or two protagonists, the depiction of life in an often geographically undefined, small-scale parochial or domestic middle-class environment, with a prerogative of women, in which kinship -, romantic - and social relationships play a key role. Those three types of relationships and their potential overlap also constitute the core narrative elements of soap opera. The main underlying storylines are motivated by those elements and are interwoven with eachother to bring about the open-ended episodes as part of a continuous narrative. Other traditional characteristics of that form are that it is almost invariably set in the present and the overall organization of the narrative time occurs largely in analogy with the progress of time in real life (though there are also generic developments, which subvert those features).

Coronation Street has brought about a variation of the traditional soap opera features by presenting for the first time a group of working-class, or at least lower class characters in a distinct urban milieu as core dramatis personae. The traditional soap opera prerogative of women was realized in *Coronation Street* in reference to the - by now almost stereotypical - image of the in comparison with her middle-class counterpart more forward and outspoken working-class woman. Like other Social Realist elements in the serial, that image was also coined by the fictional and factual writing on the working class at the time of the serial's commencement. Until today the serial features a core of strong, assertive and at times aggressive female characters, who even under the new set-up rarely have more than conventional good looks.

106

However, the most important element by which *Coronation Street* today distingishes itself from most other continuous serials with a traditionally strong tendency to melodrama, is the comedy.

As has been suggested by the authors of the *Television Monograph: Coronation Street*, the gender conflict is one of the central sources of narrative tension in the serial, another one being the inside/outside opposition in the community and its relation to the outside world. Those types of conflict have always been more prevailing than the class conflict. In fact, as Paterson and Stewart's analysis of the 1978 strike episodes reveals, the class conflict is mitigated by the two other types of conflicts.

Besides, the category of social class has always been blurred in the serial. For, the programme ever since it started has rarely featured characters who belong to the industrial working-class proper. Instead, the majority of characters have always been petty bourgeois, the rest could perhaps be described as 'respectable working-class'.

This has mainly been attributed to the soap opera prerogative of diologue in a domestic and parochial milieu, which seems to require that most characters' places of work are situated within the serial community. The lack of industrial workers is then due to the fact that industrial work places normally do not fulfill that requirement. That generic tendency also matches some concepts and images conveyed by the Social Realist novels, plays and films of the late fifties and by Richard Hoggart's book *The Uses of Literacy* (1957).

In his partially autobiographical account on working-class life and culture in the North of England Hoggart describes the working-class family and community as main generators of a distinct working-class culture. What he largely omits, however, is the sphere of work and the political organizations of the working class. This also applies to most of the Social Realist fictional writing of that time, except that the books, plays and films for generic reasons rather focus on individuals than on a group of people.

Coronation Street, similar to the above-mentioned literature on the working-class, seems to have always represented the large and ill-defined mass of 'common people', rather than any distinct social and economic category of the working class.

Nevertheless, despite such limitations, it is still true that the serial has offered unusual patterns of identification in a medium which is up to now dominated by the representation of middle-class life styles.
In a number of respects *Coronation Street* seems to be the result of the spill-over of a cultural trend which received a very broad reception, into a popular television genre. Although the Socialist leanings of the Bernstein family may have also played a role, it was mainly because other Social Realist narratives had evoked an interest in the affairs of the working class that a Social Realist soap opera could be

produced. Within that cultural climate could *Coronation Street* become popular and after some time self-perpetuating.

Although today the central setting of the serial, a working-class terrace, has long lost its typicality in a working-class life style, the programme in its title appears to still insist on mytonymic typicality. Yet, it seems to be less a working-class community that has an affinity to real life (though remnants of the milieu still exist today, especially in the North of England) which the programme is about today. Rather, it is the essence of a strong community, which can survive despite 'blows' from outside and despite inside controversies which is central and which seems to have even a national significance in Britain.

Nevertheless, the serial in line with a more general tradition of Social Realist television drama in Britain, seems to have opened a cultural space. That cultural space could be occupied and expanded by a serial like *EastEnders*, which starting in 1985 has likewise featured a community of lower class people in a distinct urban milieu. The survey conducted by the BBC prior to the production of *EastEnders* reflects that the predispositions of British viewers towards a possible new soap opera were influenced by *Coronation Street*.

In the same year a similar cultural space seems not to have existed in Germany, when *Lindenstraße* was conceived. Unlike *EastEnders*, the German serial could not draw on any indigenous programme tradition of a continuous long-running serial whatsoever. Facing an audience that was not even very familiar with the more general conventions of the soap opera genre, the producers chose a more neutral social setting in order not to risk popularity. Furthermore, the German serial also employs stylistic devices (such as music and the occasional depiction of picturesque landscapes) that differ from those of the main Social Realist soap operas in Britain. Apparently, the Social Realist narrative structure and conventions had to be adapted to the specific predispositions of German viewers and to a German production background.

In summary of the close-analysis of the two 1983 episodes featuring the Deirdre/Ken marriage crisis, it can be said that the systematic film analysis heightens the insight into the modes of plot construction, narrative form and structure of *Coronation Street* at that particular time. It also helps to understand that the meaning of one element in the narrative depends very much upon its position in the overall structure of the television discourse. Thus, Ken's assault on Deirdre, for example, acquires a different meaning through the distancing effect of the high camera angle in the shot immediately following.

Generally, it is interesting to note that camera style, particularly in the second episode, seems to replace some of the functions which in other film narratives are fulfilled by music, namely the creation of atmosphere. The effect of that device seems somewhat wooden, but, as with the more general rules of the serial narrative, comprehending such scenes relies very much upon the viewers acquaintance with them.

On a syntagmatic level the storylines of the two episodes would by any literary standards be characterized as conventional and even trivial and the solutions common-place with little psychological insight.
From a paradigmatic perspective much of the characters' actions and reactions within these plots resemble rituals enacted in the well-defined space of the *Street*. Thus, the Deirdre/Ken/Mike constellation in the *Coronation Street* narrative is not new but has been suggested before, when Deirdre had to choose between Ken and Mike some years before and is in fact to be reworked in subsequent years. Nevertheless, there are variations in the ritual or rather in the paradigmatic units employed such as, for instance, Ken's assault on Deirdre.

On an ideological level, the expression of a dominant moral code by Ken is, however, subverted by reflections in other storylines and through the knowledge that due to the demand for new storylines the normal order of things in a continuous serial is one of unstable marital relationships. After all that convention is also reflected in Ken and Deirdre's previous and subsequent 'curricula vitae'.

The portrayal of class and gender in these episodes seems to rely very much on a common-sense view of these categories.
The representation of gender is marked by an overall image of female strength, explicitly in the first episode, more implicitly in the second episode under consideration. However, that image is mainly established through the use of stereotypes of female strength, coined in a male-dominated society (but also adopted by a lot of women).

In its representation of the class aspect these two episodes - like other episodes - convey a very blurred and apolitical concept of social class. The Ogden-storyline, which seems to suggest the commonsense conclusion that it is people's own fault if they end up like the Ogdens, reveals that this sort of commonsense attitude - like the stereotypical image of female strength - is clearly marked by the dominant social consciousness of a mainly middle-class oriented capitalist society (which is, however, shared by many lower class people). The popularity of the two episodes (and of the programme as a whole) seems to rely on the reassurance of the main elements of the prevailing social believes.
However, the example of Eddie Yeats who with a former criminal record is in the two episodes suggested as an example of thrift and industry, reflects that a consistent reassurance of dominant social - and moral codes are undermined by the narrative excess of the endless soap opera text and the many layers of significational possibilities which it accumulates.

Another source of subversion of the Realism in the two episodes, as in the programme in general, is the comedy. Eddie Yeats and the Ogdens are caricatures and any meaning engendered through those characters cannot be taken too seriously. Thus, the moralistic tone of the Barlow storyline is undermined by the parody in the storyline about the Ogdens and their ridiculously stable marriage. Besides, Bet Lynch's remark in the first episode that "this place has no connections" can not only be understood as a social critical remark but also as one of the serial's customary elements of self-parody. It would then mean 'this place has no connections with the real world' and undermine the serial's claim to Realism.

In fact, a lot of the enjoyment which viewers did probably derive from those two episodes can be related to a playful handling of conventions which the serial seems to implicitly encourage while explicitly relying on conventional narrative strategies.

Generally speaking, the range of significational possibilities which the serial offers to its audience, seem to be polarized between a reading as straight forward Realist text on one side and on the other side a detached and purely aesthetic perception of the serial as an overconventionalized narrative, such as has been exemplified by the Camp vision. In between those two poles the narrative allows a variety of serious and less serious readings.

As viewers in another context were found to "commute with considerable ease between a referential and a purely fictional reading"[2], it is likely that the different ways in which viewers relate to *Coronation Street* also overlap, depending on the category of viewer (defined according to demographic and cognitive characteristics) and the situation of viewing.

As a concluding remark from a German author, the suggestion may be granted that one of the programme's long-term merits is perhaps the very fact that a group of urban 'common people' became a cherished emblem of British society, which otherwise seems to be so conscious of social distinctions.

---

[2] Ellen Seiter, Hans Borchers, Gabriele Kreutzner and Eva-Maria Warth, Don't Treat Us Like We Are Stupid: Towards An Ethnography of Soap Opera Viewers. In: Ellen Seiter et al. (eds.), op. cit.

BIBLIOGRAPHY AND RESOURCE LIST

1. Study Guides

Film and Television Handbook 1991, edited by British Film Institute, (London, 1990).

Oliver, Elizabeth (ed.), *Researcher's Guide to British Film and TV Collections.* (British University Film Council Ltd. (n.p.), 1981).

Teaching Coronation Street, (British Film Institute Educational Department, London, 1983).

2. Dictionaries

Dictionary of Literary Terms, edited by J.A. Guddon,((Penguin) Harmondsworth, 1977).

Lexikon zur populären Kultur II: Unterhaltung, edited by Georg Seeplen and Bernt Kling, ((rororo) Hamburg, 1977).

Melnau, Rudolf, *Synonymik der englischen Sprache,* (Frankfurt, 1964).

Oakey, Virginia, *Dictionary of Film and Television Terms,* ((Barnes and Noble Books) New York, Philadelphia, London and Mexico City, 1983).

The Dickens Dictionary: A Key to the Plots and Characters in the Tales of Charles Dickens, edited by Gilbert A. Pierce (with additions by William A. Heeler), (New York, 1965).

3. Primary Material

The Broadcasting Act 1990 published by Her Majesty's Stationary Office.

The Report on Broadcasting of the Pilkington Committee, (London, 1962) publ. by HMSO.

The First Five Episodes of Coronation Street (December 1960)

The Episode of 9 February 1961

The Episode of 25 December 1961

The Episode of 11 July 1962

The Episode of 12 December 1962

The Episode of 23 December 1964

The Episode of 7 April 1975

Three Episodes of 1977

Four Episodes of 1980

Three Episodes of 1981

Five Episodes of 1982

Twenty-five Episodes of 1983

Eight Episodes of 1984

Two Episodes of 1985

One Episode of 1988

Five Episodes of 1990

Broadcasters' Audience Research Board, *Trends in Television,* (February and April, 1985)

Broadcasters' Audience Research Board, *April 1985 Survey of Viewers' Opinions.*

Broadcasters' Audience Research Board, January 1991 *Survey of Viewers' Opinons.*

The TAM, JICTAR and BARB Audience Research Records from 1960-1985 and the BARB records of 1990.

4.   Secondary Literature

Allsop, Kenneth, *The Angry Decade: A Survey of The Cultural Revolt of The Nineteen-Fifties,* (London, 3rd ed., 1964).

Alvarado, Manuel and Edward Buscombe, *Hazell: The Making of a TV Series,* (London, 1978).

Armes, Roy *A Critical History of British Cinema,* (London, 1978).

Bark, Joachim, "Der Kreistanz ums Triviale: Probleme der Forschung und des Unterrichts", in: Annaria Rucktaschel and Hans-Dieter Zimmermann (eds.), *Trivialliteratur,* (Munich, 1976), pp 10-29.

Barr, Charles, *Ealing Comedies,* (London, 1977).

Barthes, Roland, *Elemente der Semiologie,* (Frankfurt, 2nd ed., 1981).

Barthes, Roland, "The Rhetoric of the Image", *Working Papers for Cultural Studies,* (Spring, 1971), pp. 37-50.

Barthes, Roland, *Mythologies*, (London, 1972).

Bennett, Tony et al. (eds.), *Popular Culture: Past and Present,* (London, 1982).

Bennett, Tony et al. (eds.), *Popular Telelvision and Film,* (London, 1981).

Blackwell, Trevor, "The History of a Working-Class Methodist Chapel", *Working Papers in Cultural Studies 5,* (Spring, 1974), pp. 65-83.

Brandt, George W. (ed.), *British Television Drama,* (Cambridge, London, New York, New Rochelle, Melbourne, Sydney, 1981).

Brown, Mary Ellen (ed.), *Television and Women's Culture*, (London, New Delhi, Newbury Park, CA, 1990).

Brunsdon, Charlotte, "Crossroads: Notes on Soap Cpera", *Screen* 22,4 (Winter, 1981).

Buckingham, David, *Public Secrets: EastEnders and Its Audience*, (London, 1987).

Buckman, Peter, *All For Love: A Study in Soap Opera,* (London, 1984).

Buscombe, Edward (ed.), *Granada: The First 25 Years,* (BFI Dossier Number 9), (London, 1981).

Cantor, Muriel G. and Suzanne Pingree, *The Soap Opera* ((Sage) Beverly Hills, London, New Delhi, 1983).

Cassata, Mary and Thomas Skill (eds.), *Life on Daytime Televsion*: *Tuning-In American Serial Drama*, ((Ablex) Norwood, NJ, 1983).

Chambers, Ian, "Roland Barthes: Structuralism/Semiotics", *Working Papers in Cultural Studies 6*, pp. 49-70.

Clarke, John et al. (eds.), *Working-Class Culture: Studies in History and Theory*, (2nd ed., London, 1980).

Collins, Richard and Vincent Porter, *Television Monongraph: WDR and the Arbeiterfilm - Fassbinder Ziewer and others*, (London, 1981).

Conrad, Peter, *The Medium and Its Manners*, (London and Henley, 1982).

Coolidge, Archibald C., *Charles Dickens As Serial Novelist*, (Iowa State Univ. Press Ames, 1967).

Day-Lewis, Sean, *One Day in The Life of Television*, (London, Glasgow, Toronto, Sydney and Auckland, 1989).

Delaney, Shelagh, *A Taste of Honey*, (2nd ed., London, 1959).

Dellig, Manfred, *Bonanza und Co.: Fernsehen als Unterhaltung und Politik - Eine kritische Bestandsaufnahme,((rororo)* Hamburg, 1977).

Durzak, Manfred, "Kojak, Columbo und deutsche Kollegen: Überlegungen zum Fernseh-Serial", In: Helmut Kreuzer und Karl Prümm (eds.), *Fernsehsendungen und ihre Formen*, (Stuttgart, 1979), pp. 71-93.

Dyer, Richard et al., *Television Monograph: Coronation Street*, ((BFI) London, 1981).

Eaton, Mick, "Television Situation Comedy", *Screen* Vol. 19/4, 1979-1980.

Eco, Umberto, "Towards a Semiotic Enquiry into the Television Message", *Working Papers in Cultural Studies 3*, (Autumn, 1972), pp. 103-121.

Edmondson, Madeleine and David Rounds, *From Mary Noble to Mary Hartman: The Complete Soap Opera Book*, (New York, 1976).

Enzensherger, Hans Magnus, "Baukasten zu einer Theorie der Medien", *Kursbuch 20*, (1970), pp. 159-186.

Faulstich, Werner (ed.), *Kritische Stichwörter zur Medienwissenschaft*, (Munich, 1979).

Faulstich, Werner und Ingeborg, *Modelle der Filmanalyse,* (Munich, 1977).

Ferguson, Marjorie (ed.), *New Communication Technologies and The Public Interest: Comparative Perspectives on Policy and Research*, ((Sage) London, Beverly Hills and New Delhi, 1986).

Fiske, John, *Television Culture*, (London and New York, 1987).

Fiske, John and John Hartley, *Reading Television,* (2nd ed., London and New York, 1980).

Fiske, John, Television Culture, ((Methuen) London and New York, 1987).

Foltin, Hans-Friedrich, "Presentation of the Working World in the Mass Media in the Federal Republic of Germany", in: *Labor, the Working Class and the Media,* (Norwood, 1983).

Frey-Vor, Gerlinde, "Die Lindenstraße - ein Gegenstand für den Deutschunterricht?". *Der Deutschunterricht* 6, 1990.

Frey-Vor, Gerlinde, *Soap Operas and Telenovelas, Communication Research Trends* 10, 1+2 (1990).

Gill, Davies, "Teaching about Narrative", *Screen Education* Vol. 29, (Winter, 1978-79).

Gunter, Barrie and Michael Svennevig, *Behind and in Front of The Screen: Television's Involvement with Family Life*, (London and Paris, 1987).

Hall, Stuart et al. (eds.), *Culture, Media, Language: Working Papers in Cultural Studies 1972-79,* ((Hutchinson) 2nd ed., London, 1981).

Hall, Stuart, "Encoding and Decoding in the Television Discourse", *Stencilled Occasional Papers* (1973), (Centre for Contemporary Cultural Studies, Birmingham).

Hall, Stuart, "Television as a Medium and its Relation to Culture", *Stencilled Occasional Papers* (1975), (Centre for Contemporary Cultural Studies, Birmingham).

Herzog Massing, Herta, Decoding Dallas: Comparing American and German Viewers. In: Arthur Asa Berger (ed.), *Television in Society*, (New Brunswick, NJ, 1987).

Hobson, Dorothy, *Crossroads: The Drama of a Soap Opera,* (London, 1982).

Hoggart, Richard, *The Uses of Literacy, (10th ed.,* (Penguin) Harmondsworth, 1968).

Hoggart, Richard (ed.), *Your Sunday Paper,* (London, 1967), pp. 20-29.

Hoggart, Richard, "TV in a Free Society", *Contrast* 2, (1962-63).

Hood, Stuart, *On Television,* (2nd ed., (Pluto press) London, 1983).

Kaminsky, St.M. and J.H. Mahan (eds.), *American Television Genres,* (Chicago, 1985).

Internationales Handbuch für Rundfunk und Fernsehen 1990, edited by Hans-Bredow-Institut (Hamburg, 1990).

Intintoli, Michael James, *Taking Soaps Seriously: The World of Guiding Light,* (New York, 1984).

James, Louis, *Fiction for the Working Man 1830- 1850,* (London, 1963).

Johnston, Sheila, *Crossroads: Approaches to Popular Television Fiction,* ((n.p.), 1981).

Katzman, Nathan, "Seifenopern im amerikanischen Fernsehen: Was geschieht überhaupt in ihnen?", in: Dieter Prokop (ed.), *Massenkommunikationsforschung: Produktanalysen,* (Frankfurt, 1977), pp. 85-99.

Kershaw, H.V., *Coronation Street: Early Days,* ((Granada/Mayflower) Aylesburg, 1976).

Kershaw, H.V., *The Street where I Live,* ((Granada) London, 1969).

Kershaw, John, "Synthetic Gossip", *Contrast* (Summer, 1964).

Kettle, Arnold, "Dickens and the Popular Tradition", *Zeitschrift für Anglistik und Amerikanistik* (9/1961).

Klagsbrunn, Marta Maria, *Brasiliens Fernsehserien, Telenovelas: Die allabendliche Faszination,* ((Brasilienkunde Verlag) Mettingen, 1987).

Knilli, Friedrich, *Literaturwissenschaft - Medienwissenschaft,* (Heidelberg, 1977).

Knilli, Friedrich, *Die Unterhaltung der deutschen Fernsehfamilie,* (Berlin, 1971).

Kuchenbuch, Thomas, *Filmanalyse: Theorien, Modelle, Kritik,* (Cologne, 1978).

Lazarsfeld, Paul F. and Frank Stanton (eds.), *Radio Research 1942-1943,* (New York, 1944).

Lévi-Strauss, Claude, *Mythos und Bedeutung* (Vorträge), (Frankfurt, 1980).

Lévi-Strauss, Claude, *The Naked Man: Indroduction to Science of Mythology 4* (New York, 1981).

Lévi-Strauss, Claude, *Structural Analysis of Linguistics and Anthropology I*, (London, 1968).

Lewis, Peter, "Z-Cars", *Contrast* (1/1961-62).

Liebes, Tamar, "Cultural Differences in The Retelling of Television Fiction". Critical *Studies in Mass Communication*, Vol. 5,4 (December, 1988).

Livingstone, Sonia, Viewers' Interpretation of Soap Opera Characters. In: Philipp Drummond and Richard Paterson (eds.), *Television and Its Audience: International Research Perspectives*, (London, 1988).

Lull, James (ed.), *World Families Watch Television*, (London, New Delhi, Newbury Park, CA, 1988.

Marles, Vivien and Nadine Nohr, *EastEnders*: The Research Contribution. In: *Annual Review of BBC Broadcasting Research Findings* Nr. 12 ((BBC Data Publications) London, 1986), p. 69.

Mattelart, Michèle and Armand Mattelart, *Le Carnaval Des Images: La Fiction Bresilienne*, (Paris, 1987).

McCabe, Colin, "Realism and The Cinema: Notes on Some Brechtian Theses", *Screeen* Vol. 15, 2 (1974).

McQuail, Denis and Sven Windahl, *Communication Models for the Study of Mass Communication,* (London and New York, 1981).

Merten, Klaus, *Inhaltsanalyse: Einführung in Theorie, Methode und Praxis,* (Opladen, 1983).

Mikos, Lothar, Familienserien - Familienbilder. In: Dieter Baacke and Jürgen Lauffer (eds.), *Familien im Mediennetz*, (Opladen, 1988).

Modleski, Tania, *Loving with A Vengeance: Mass Produced Fantasies for Women*, (Hamden, CT, 1982).

Monaco, James, *How to Read a Film: The Art, Technology, Language, History and Theory of Film and Media,* (2nd ed., New York, Oxford, 1981).

Morley, David, *Family Television: Cultural Power and Domestic Leisure*, (London, 1986).

Munro, Colin R., *Television, Censorship and the Law,* ((Saxon House) London, 1979).

Neubourg, Victor E., *Popular Literature: A History and Guide,* ((Penguin) Harmondsworth, 1977).

Newcomb, Horace (ed.), *Television: The Critical View,* (3rd ed., New York and Oxford, 1982).

Orwell, George, *The Road to Wigan Pier,* (20th ed., (Penguin) Harmondsworth, 1981).

Paech, Joachim (ed.), *Film - und Fernsehsprache 1,* (Frankfurt, Berlin, Munich, 1976).

Prokop, Dieter (ed.), *Massenkommunikationsforschung 1: Produktion,* (Frankfurt, 1972).

Propp, Vladlmir, *Die Morphologie des Märchens,* ((Suhrkamp) Frankfurt, 1975).

Roberts, Robert, *The Classic Slum* (5th ed. (Penguin) Harmondsworth, 1980).

Rössler, Patrick, Medienskripten Vol. I: *Dallas und Schwarzwaldklinik: Eine Programmstudie über Soap Operas,* ((R. Fischer Verlag) Munich, 1988).

Rogge, Jan-Uwe, Tagträume oder warum Familienserien so beliebt sind. Zur Geschichte, Machart und psycho-sozialen Funktion von Familienserien im deutschen Fernsehen. In: *Medienpolitik,* edited by Landeszentrale für politische Bildung Baden-Württemberg, (Stuttgart, 1987).

Rosenberg von, Ingrid, "Militancy, Anger and Resignation: Alternative Moods in the Working-Class Novel of the 1950s and Early 1960s", in: H. Gustav Klaus (ed.), *The Socialist Novel in Britain: Towards the Recovery of a Tradition,* (Brighton, 1982).

Seiter, Ellen et al. (eds.), *Remote Control: Television, Audiences and Cultural Power,* (London, New York, 1990).

Sendall, Bernhard, *History of ITV Vol. 2 (1958-68),* (London and Basingstoke, 1983).

Schanze, Helmut, "Fernsehserien: Ein literaturwissenschaftlicher Gegenstand?", *Lili* Vol 2, 6 (1972), pp. 79 - 94.

Silj, Alessandro et al., *East of Dallas: The European Challenge to American Television,* (London, 1988).

Silverstone, Roger, *The Message of Television: Myth and Narrative in Contemporary Culture,* (London, 1981).

Sontag, Susan, *Against Interpretation (and other Essays),* (6th ed., New York, 1966)

Stedman, Raymond William, *The Serials: Suspense and Drama by Installment,* (Norman Oklahoma, 1971).

Taylor, John Russel, *Anger and After: A Guide to the New British Drama,* (2nd ed., Fakenham, 1969).

Taylor, Laurie and Bob Mullan, *Uninvited Guests: The Intimate Secrets of of Television and Radio,* (London, 1986).

Thompson, Denys (ed.), *Discrimination and Popular Culture,* (5th ed., (Penguin) Harmondsworth, 1970).

Thompson, E.P., *The Making of the English Working Class,* (4th ed., London, 1965).

Tulloch, John and Albert Moran, A Country Practice: Quality Soap, ((Currency Press) Sydney, 1986).

Walker, Alexander, *Hollywood England: The British Film Industry in the Sixties,* (London, 1974).

Warner, W. Lloyd and William E. Henry, "The Radio Day-Time Serial: A Symbolic Analysis". *Genetic Psychology Monographs*, Vol. 37, pp. 3-71.

Warren, Tony, *I Was Ena Sharples' Father,* (London, 1969).

Weatherby, W.J., "Granada's Camino Real", *Contrast* 1, 1962.

Wichterich, Christa, *Unsere Nachbarn heute Abend - Familienserien im Fernsehen,* (Frankfurt, New York, 1979).

Williams, Raymond, *Television: Technology and Cultural Form,* (4th ed., (Fontana) London, 1974).

Wilson, Harold, *Pressure Group: The Campaign for Commercial Television in England,* (New Brunswick, 1961).

Young, Michael and Peter Willmot, *Family and Kinship in East London,* (16th ed., (Penguin) Harmondsworth, 1980).

5. Newspaper and Magazine Articles and Unpublished Material

Culverhouse, Diane, Diary of A Storyline Writer. (Unpublished material from the British Film Institute project 'One Day in The Life of Television')

Day-Lewis, Sean, "Back where it all began". *The Scotsman*, 3 December 1990.

Dunkley, Christopher, "Brand New Programmes Kick off The Year". *Financial Times* 16. 1. 1988.

Dyer, Richard et al., "Soap Opera and Women", (Paper held at the Edinburgh International Television Festival 1977).

Forster, Peter, "Down Coronation Street", *Spectator,* 3 January 1962.

Hall, Willis, Soap with a lasting lather". *Observer* 9 December 1990.

Harding, Sarah, Diary of A Director. (Unpublished material from the British Film Instute project 'One Day in The Life of Television')

Hill, Barry, Diary of A Storyline writer. (Unpublished material from the British Film Instute project 'One Day in The Life of Television')

Interviews with producer Mervyn Watson, *Coronation Street* press officer Graham King and Granada public affairs officer Hellen Webb.

Mosley, Brian, Diary of An Actor. (Unpublished material from the British Film Instute project 'One Day in The Life of Television')

N.N., "Mean Steet: Putting the boot in to EastEnders". *Daily Mirror* 4 February 1989.

N.N., "Roy pays homage to the Rovers Return". *The Independent* 27 August 1990, p. 15.

N.N., "Strategies for the Unemployed: Surviving the Dole", *Face* (1/1986).

Purves, Libby, "The Street with a tender touch". *The Times Saturday Review* 8 December 1990.

BFI Summaries of the *Coronation Street* episodes of 19 and 21 December 1988.

The TV Times Souvenir Album: Coronation Street, (London, 1981).

The TV Times of 8 - 14 December 1990 with *Coronation Street* specials.

Thornber, R., "Why Coronation Street Will Never Be the Susie Hush Show", *Guardian,* 13 December 1974, p.8.

Waterman, Jack, "Folk Are Not Daft", *Listener,* 16 September 1976.

Coronation Street (Ken/Deirdre Crisis)

The Episode was transmitted on the 17th of February 1983

\- Visual Segments								
Sequence				Subsequence (Scene)		Shot		
Nr	Dur	Setting	Personae	Nr	Plot	Nr	Dur	Objects
0	19 sec	opening sequence: Outside of Coronation Street				1		roofs of working-class terraces - on the horizon a factory and tower blocks
						2		chimneys on roofs
						3		houses of CS
						4		a cat on a roof
						5		back-yards of CS
						6		the row of houses in CS
1	1 m 23 sec	First, the lane behind the back-yards of CS. (it is a narrow, dreary, and on this day wet lane. It is situated between the back-yards of CS and those of another street. On both sides are dustbins and sacks with rubbish.)	Eddie Yeats and Chalkie, another dustman Elsie Tanner, Suzie Birchall and Eddie's girlfriend Marion	1	Eddie and his collegue come walking up the lane, emptying dustbins. In front of Elsie Tanner's back-yard they stop and talk. Eventually Eddie enters Elsie's house via the backdoor.	1	29 sec	Eddie and Chalkie are walking towards the camera. They stop and talk. Then Eddie hands Chalkie a plastic sack filled with rubbish, and leaves. Chalkie continues emptying bins.
		Secondly, Elsie Tanner's house, or rather her kitchen living-room. In that room there is a green kitchen unit and a rectangular table with chairs. On the wall there are two prints.		2	Elsie, Suzie and Marion are having breakfast. Eddie joins them. Suzie treats Eddie in a spiteful way.	1	3 sec	The three women at a breakfast table
						2	2 sec	Marion turns her head towards the back-door. Elsie is also visible, she is reading a newspaper.
						3	3 sec	Suzie alone
						4	17 sec	Marion and Elsie
								Eddie appears behind Marion's back

		Acoustic and Linguistic Segments	
Shot		**Sound effect**	**Dialogue**
Type/camera movem./cam. angle			
extreme long	bird-eye view	signature tune	
full	eye-level		
establishing	bird-eye view		
close-up	eye-level		
long	bird-eye view		
long	eye-level		
from long to medium	eye-level	normal back-ground noise eg. steps in puddles and rustling with plastic sacks	Eddie Yeats: "'ey, Chalkie just chew the cud for five minutes, will you. I'm nippin' in here for a cuppa." Chalkie: "You're not goin' in there for no cuppa." Eddie: "But what else?" Chalkie: "Wha' three women in there, probably semi-naked. Do me a favour..." Eddie: "Chalkie to the pure in heart the female form might just as well be a concrete mixer .... here (hands him the plastic sack)".
establishing	eye-level	normal back-ground noise,	
medium (small)	eye-level	eg. clicking of door,	Eddie (off screen): "'xcuse me, anybody want any help with their corsets?"
close-up	eye-level		Suzie: "Oh, not 'im again ... d'ya 'ave to 'ave breakfast with a flaming binman?"
medium	eye-level		Marion (still chewing her cereals): "It's not just a flaming binman. It's my Eddie!"
camera moves up a little			

Visual Segments								
Sequence				Subsequence (Scene)		Shot		
Nr	Dur	Setting	Personae	Nr	Plot	Nr	Dur	Objects
1		continued		2	continued	4		Eddie near Marion, talking to her. Marion gets up with the empty tea-pot. Eddie sits down on her chair. He greets Elsie who looks up from behind her tabloid paper. He also greets Suzie.
						5	2 sec	Suzie looking daggers at him.
						6	7 sec	Eddie, taking off his gloves - Marion standing diagonally behind him.
						7	3 sec	Suzie
						8	2 sec	Eddie - Marion is still behind him
						9	1 sec	Suzie
						10	3 sec	Eddie looks up from her tabloid paper and takes a glance at Eddie
						11	1 sec	Eddie
						12	2 sec	Suzie
						13	5 sec	Eddie - Marion brings the teapot - Elsie can also be seen
						14	2 sec	Suzie

		Acoustic and Linguistic Segments
Shot	**sound effect**	**Dialogue**
Type/camera movem./cam. angle		
medium zoom(in) eye-level camera moves down and pans slightly to the right	normal b. g. n.	Eddie: "'ey the three fellows I've just seen leavin'. So that's allright here if I play me cards right." Marion: (grins) "I s'ppose you want a cup of tea, don't you?" Eddie: "Well, it crossed my mind ..." Marion: "Come sit down!" Eddie: "(cheerfully) Else!" Elsie: "(tired) Morning ..." Eddie: "(just as cheerfully) Suse!"
close-up eye-level		
medium (small)		Eddie: "'ey we 've had a great mornin' , me and the lads. You know we're half way through our quarter and it is not eight o' clock. I mean, 'ow many people can say they 've cleaned up a corner of the world before it is not eight o'clock."
close-up eye-level		Suzie: "You mean you 've been humping grotty dustbins."
medium (small) eye-level		Eddie: "Close around 200 as a matter of fact."
close-up eye-level		Suzie: "(indignant) And then you come walzing in here?"
medium (small) eye-level		Eddie: "(off screen at first) I thought I've done me work for the community and I'd come and spread a bit of bonhomie among me friends."
medium (small) eye-level		
close-up eye-level		Suzie: "Pph, is that what you call it?"
medium (small) eye-level zoom (out) medium	the sound of tea being poured	Eddie: "Don't worry Suse, you'll get to love me, everybody does!" Marion: "An' that's a fact!"
close-up eye-level		

	Visual Segments						

| Sequence | | | | Subsequence (Scene) | | Shot | |

Nr	Dur	Setting	Personae	Nr	Plot	Nr	Dur	Objects
2	1 m 52 sec	Ken and Deirdre Barlow's and Albert Tatlock's house. In this house the kitchen is separate from the living-room. The living-room displays old-fashioned cosiness. It is decorated with flowered wallpaper and has a fireplace with open fire. On the mantelpiece there is an old clock. The room is furnished with a huge, old sideboard, a large oval table, an old-fashioned sofa, chairs and arm-chairs. In one corner there is a television, in another a small cupboard with books.	Deirdre and Barlow and Emily Bishop	1	Ken and Deirdre Barlow are also having breakfast. They talk about Ken's not getting the job for which he applied. Eventually Ken gets up and walks into the hall. When he passes the front door, there is a knock on the door. It is Emily Bishop who wants to return a drawing book that their little daughter Tracey left at her house.	1	2 sec	Ken's hands cutting toast on a plate
						2	2 sec	Deirdre
						3	6 sec	Ken's hands again - then his face and shoulders
						4	2 sec	Deirdre looking at him silently
						5	15 sec	Ken - first thinking then talking - then getting up and opening the door to the hall
						6	18 sec	Ken walking into the hall - answering the door to let Emily in - going upstairs. Emily holding up Tracey's book - walking a few steps into the hall - hesitating for a moment then going through the door of the living-room
				2	Ken lets Emily in and goes upstairs. Emily enters the living-room where Deirdre is. She returns Tracey's book. Before she leaves, she tries to talk about the Deirdre/Mike affair.	1	2 sec	Emily (frontal) entering the room - approaching Deirdre who is sitting with her back to the camera
						2	2 sec	Deirdre
						3	11 sec	Emily coming nearer, holding up Tracey's book. Deirdre again with back to camera.

	Acoustic and Linguistic Segments	
Shot	sound effect	Dialogue
Type/camera movem./cam. angle		
detail	normal back-ground noise	
extreme close-up eye-level		
from detail to close-up camera moves up and zoom (out) eye-level		Ken: "I wonder if Alf managed to find out anything last night."
close-up eye-level		
close-up of his face then part of his back as he is getting up eye-level		Ken: "It shouldn't be too difficult somebody knows why I was turned down .... I'd been good at it too. I'd been very good. I know I would."
medium (large) pan to right eye-level	knock at the front door	
pan to left medium		Emily: "Oh, good morning. I've got Tracey's dinosaur book ...." Ken: "Deirdre is in the living-room."
from medium (large) to medium zoom eye-level		Emily: "Deirdre ...."
close-up eye-level		Deirdre: "Hello!"
medium eye-level	normal back-ground noise	Emily: "Tracey left her dinosaur book last night ... as I thought she might need it at school. I'd try to give it to Ken .... but he was ... eh ... in a hurry."

					Visual Segments			

<table>
<tr><th colspan="4">Sequence</th><th colspan="3">Subsequence (Scene)</th><th colspan="3">Shot</th></tr>
<tr><th>Nr</th><th>Dur</th><th>Setting</th><th>Personae</th><th>Nr</th><th colspan="2">Plot</th><th>Nr</th><th>Dur</th><th>Objects</th></tr>
<tr><td>2</td><td></td><td>continued</td><td></td><td>2</td><td colspan="2">continued</td><td>4</td><td>4 sec</td><td>Deirdre (profile)</td></tr>
<tr><td></td><td></td><td></td><td></td><td></td><td colspan="2"></td><td>5</td><td>10 sec</td><td>Emily turning round to go but then she hesitates and turns back to Deirdre.</td></tr>
<tr><td></td><td></td><td></td><td></td><td></td><td colspan="2"></td><td>6</td><td>1 sec</td><td>Deirdre</td></tr>
<tr><td></td><td></td><td></td><td></td><td></td><td colspan="2"></td><td>7</td><td>2 sec</td><td>Emily</td></tr>
<tr><td></td><td></td><td></td><td></td><td></td><td colspan="2"></td><td>8</td><td>3 sec</td><td>Deirdre</td></tr>
<tr><td></td><td></td><td></td><td></td><td></td><td colspan="2"></td><td>9</td><td>4 sec</td><td>Emily</td></tr>
<tr><td></td><td></td><td></td><td></td><td></td><td colspan="2"></td><td>10</td><td>2 sec</td><td>Deirdre</td></tr>
<tr><td></td><td></td><td></td><td></td><td></td><td colspan="2"></td><td>11</td><td>5 sec</td><td>Emily</td></tr>
<tr><td></td><td></td><td></td><td></td><td></td><td colspan="2"></td><td>12</td><td>2 sec</td><td>Deirdre</td></tr>
<tr><td></td><td></td><td></td><td></td><td></td><td colspan="2"></td><td>13</td><td>2 sec</td><td>Emily</td></tr>
<tr><td></td><td></td><td></td><td></td><td></td><td colspan="2"></td><td>14</td><td>5 sec</td><td>Deirdre</td></tr>
<tr><td></td><td></td><td></td><td></td><td></td><td colspan="2"></td><td>15</td><td>5 sec</td><td>Emily</td></tr>
<tr><td></td><td></td><td></td><td></td><td></td><td colspan="2"></td><td>16</td><td>3 sec</td><td>Deirdre</td></tr>
<tr><td></td><td></td><td></td><td></td><td></td><td colspan="2"></td><td>17</td><td>2 sec</td><td>Emily turning to go</td></tr>
<tr><td></td><td></td><td></td><td></td><td></td><td colspan="2"></td><td>18</td><td>4 sec</td><td>Deirdre (profile)</td></tr>
<tr><td>3</td><td>1 m 25 sec</td><td>At Alf's corner shop

The corner-shop is not very spacious but there is room enough for the customers to move about.</td><td>Alf Roberts, Ken Barlow and Mike Baldwin</td><td>1</td><td colspan="2">Ken talks to Alf, who is an elected member of the local Council. He wants him to find out why he was not accepted for a job with the local government. He is very down. Mike ostensibly tries to cheer him up. But the entire conversation between him and Ken is ambiguous because of</td><td>1

2</td><td>2 sec

2 sec</td><td>Mike opening the door and walking in.

Ken standing in front of the counter (with back to camera), Alf is behind the counter</td></tr>
</table>

Acoustic and Linguistic Segments		
Shot	**sound effect**	**Dialogue**
Type/camera movem./cam. angle		
close-up eye-level		Deirdre: "Thanks very much, Emily. Tracey's just getting ready actually."
medium (small)		Emily: "Right ... bye! ...... Is Ken allright? He seemed ...."
close-up eye-level		Deirdre: "What?"
close-up eye-level		Emily: "Upset."
close-up eye-level		Deirdre: "He didn't get that job ..."
close-up eye-level		Emily: "Oh, no ... poor Ken."
close-up eye-level		Deirdre: "Poor us all."
close-up eye-level		Emily: "No ... but ... Are you still seeing ...?"
close-up eye-level		Deirdre: "Not so you'd noticed."
close-up eye-level		Emily: "Does that mean ...?"
close-up eye-level		Deirdre: "It means Ken's lost his job and he's been pretty upset these couple of days. That's all."
close-up eye-level		Emily: "Yes ... Will you tell him I'm very sorry!"
close-up eye-level		Deirdre: "Yeah, I will. Thanks very much, Emily."
medium eye-level		Emily: "Bye."
close-up eye-level		
medium zoom-in eye-level	bell ringing	Alf (from the off): "I tried to find out, Ken, honestly. But the fellow I was going to ask, he wasn't at the meeting last night."

medium   a slight
       pan to eye-level
       left
	normal
	back-ground
	noise
		Ken: "Well, isn't there somebody else?"

		Alf: "Well, hardly, it's supposed to be confidential, you know."

				Visual Segments				

		Sequence			Subsequence (Scene)		Shot	
Nr	Dur	Setting	Personae	Nr	Plot	Nr	Dur	Objects
3		Opposite the door there is a large counter with a till. On the right hand side near the door there is a freezer and alongside the walls there are shelves filled with boxes, glases and bottles.		1	the affair Mike has with Ken's wife Deirdre, which Ken does not know about yet.	3	10 sec	Alf with back to camera, Ken (frontal), Mike in the background at the door
						4	2 sec	Alf
						5	4 sec	Ken and Mike
						6	2 sec	Alf
						7	13 sec	Ken and Mike
						8	1 sec	Alf (silent)
						9	11 sec	Ken and Mike - Ken walking towards the door
						10	10 sce	Mike
						11	7 sec	Ken and Mike - Ken leaving the shop
				2	Mike and Alf are now alone in the shop. Mike is puzzled because of what Ken said to him before he left. They go on talking. Mike teases	1	3 sec	Mike (thinking) then turning round to Alf
						2	9 sec	Mike and Alf (seen over Alf's back left shoulder)

		sound effect	Acoustic and Linguistic Segments
Shot			**Dialogue**
Type/camera movem./cam. angle			
medium (large)	eye-level		Ken: "Confidential! Do me a favour, Alf. There's nothing confidential in that town hall. A politician is the biggest blubber-mouth in the universe, like a lot of old women."
medium (small)	eye-level		Alf: "Well, some of us can keep our mouths shut, if necessary."
medium	eye-level		Ken: "Yeah, well, when are you next likely to see ... eh ... whoever?"
medium	eye-level		Alf: "Oh, I don't know, the next day or two ... "
medium	eye-level		Ken: "Well, I'd be glad if you could find out why I was turned down. (he turns round to Mike) It beats me, it really does. I had the qualifications, had the experience and even though I say it myself the personality. Yet, they turned me down. I just don't understand."
medium (small)	eye-level		
medium pan to left	eye-level		Ken: "I was banking on that job, too. I don't know. It would have been such a shot in the arm. Oh, we all need a shot in the arm, don't we?"
medium (small)	eye-level		Mike: "But it is only one job, idn't it Kenny. I mean there is plenty of jobs floatin' around in your business, idn't there. Local government ... people retiring. I mean, it is not as if it was a steel-works or anythin'."
medium	eye-level	door bell	Ken: "The fat years have ended in local government like everywhere else, Mike! Remember Hesseltine?"
medium	eye-level		Mike: "What's he talkin' about? 'course he'll get another job, wouldn't he, eh?"
medium	eye-level		I mean, it's wheels within wheels, idn't it, eh. It's your town hall. What about all these jobs for the boys I've been 'earin' about?"

Visual Segments

		Sequence			Subsequence (Scene)		Shot	
Nr	Dur	Setting	Personae	Nr	Plot	Nr	Dur	Objects
3		continued		2	Alf by alluding to the fact that the Council has a Labour majority; Alf is not a member of the Labour party.	3	1 sec	Mike from the side - Alf frontal (pointing his finger at Mike)
						4	1 sec	Mike and Alf depicted as in shot Nr. 2
						5	3 sec	Mike and Alf depicted as in shot Nr. 3 - Alf turning to get cigars
						6	2 sec	Mike (smiling)
4	2 m 19 sec	Inside the Ogden's house In this house the kitchen is also separate from the living-room. The living-room is cheaply furnished and decorated with bad taste. On the wall which the viewer faces is a tasteless mural, depicting a flight of ducks or sea-gulls. On the wall on the right hand side there is a wall-plate, depicting Prince Charles and Lady Diana. The room is furnished with a small, old sideboard with a set of drawers, a square table, chairs and an armchair.	Stan and Hilda Ogden and Eddie Yeats	1	Stan Ogden apparently is short of money again. When he enters the living-room and discovers that he is alone in the house he starts searching for money in one of the drawers of the sideboard. But soon comes his wife Hilda.	1	28 sec	The Ogden's living-room first without anybody in. Then Stan comes in and starts rummaging in a drawer. On hearing a noice in the entrance-hall he quickly leaves the room through the kitchen.
				2	Hilda realizes that Stan has quickly left through the back-door before she came in and she complaints to Eddie Yeats who enters shortly after her. Eddie tries to divert her by showing her the statement of his and Marion's building society account with 92 Pound interest.	1	17 sec	The living-room almost as before. Stan had entered. Then Hilda appears at the door - she walks to the centre of the room and starts unbuttoning her coat. On hearing the back-door clicking, she rushes out into the kitchen. The same empty living-room as before. Eddie Yeats can be seen entering the entrance-hall. Then he comes into the living-room - hangs his jacket around the back of chair and sits down on the same chair.
						2	3 sec	Hilda returns to the living-room and talks to Eddie.
						3	2 sec	Edding sitting at the table, answers
						4	16 sec	Eddie - now seen from the back left side, still sitting - Hilda (half-profile) is standing in front of the kitchen

		Acoustic and Linguistic Segments	
Shot	sound effect		Dialogue
Type/camera movem./cam. angle			
medium eye-level	normal b. g. n.		Alf: "Now, don't you start!"
medium eye-level			Mike: "Well, you can take a joke, can't you?
medium eye-level			Give us a packet of mild cigars, will you!"
close-up eye-level	normal b. g. n.		
establishing eye-level			
pan to left zoom			Stan: "Hilda 're you up there? .... Hilda?"
medium			
	normal background noise		
establishing eye-level			
establishing eye-level			Hilda: "Stanley ....?"
medium (small) eye-level			Hilda: "Oh. I thought I heard the back-door shut ..."
medium (small) eye-level			Eddie: "We 'ave burglars ..."
establishing zoom eye-level			Hilda: "Burglars? Huh, that's a good one. What would they find to pinch in here? This place is like a pocket with a hole in it. Why it was Stanley, wasn't it. I mean
medium eye-level			

Visual Segments								
Sequence				Subsequence (Scene)		Shot		
Nr	Dur	Setting	Personae	Nr	Plot	Nr	Dur	Objects
4		continued		2	continued			door, she is taking off her coat. She walks a few steps towards the table where Eddie is just opening a letter
						5	7 sec	Eddie
						6	2 sec	Hilda (amazed)
						7	9 sec	Eddie
						8	6 sec	Hilda
						9	4 sec	Now Hilda also takes a seat at the table. Eddie is also visible. He hands the letter to Hilda.
						10	20 sec	Hilda and Eddie now seen from the back left-side. Eddie - (Half-profile) Hilda - (frontal).
						11	4 sec	Hilda and Eddie sitting like in 9.
						12	22 sec	Hilda gets up to go to the kitchen - Eddie is still at his place
								- Eddie kisses his letter.
5	1 m 35 sec	Ken and Deirdre Barlow and Tatlock's house	Ken, Deirdre and Tracey, Mike (on the phone)	1	Shortly before Ken and Tracey return Deirdre is hovering the carpet in the hall. She is interrupted by a telephone call from her lover Mike Baldwin who wants to know if she has made a decision about whether to leave	1	33 sec	Deirdre (filmed from the lobby through open door) - she is hoovering the carpet in the living-room. The telephone is in the foreground.

Shot			sound effect	Acoustic and Linguistic Segments
				Dialogue
Type/camera movem./cam. angle				
				one of his day-long tea-breaks. He 'ears us comin' and he's off like a whippet. Oh, that feller he gets worse instead of better. It's like havin' a 50-year-old truant in the 'ouse."
medium (small)		eye-level		Eddie: "'ey listen to this! 92 pound eight p., ... interest. It is nearly 100 quid for nothin'."
medium (small)		eye-level		Hilda: "You wha'?"
medium (small)		eye-level	normal back-ground noise	Eddie: "Me and Marion's building society account. Hundred pound .... eh, money does grow on trees, don't it. Would 'ave been a lot more if I hadn't lost that thousand."
medium (small)		eye-level		Hilda: "Could, could I'ave a look d'ya think? That's if it's not private-like."
medium				Eddie: "'course it's not private. Not for you Hilda. 'ere. Feast your eyes on that."
medium (small)		eye-level		Hilda: "Tsk, tsk, tsk, tsk, money in the bank!" Eddie: "Eh, building society actually." Hilda: "Oh, same thing. Oh it's right what they say, ya know ... more makes more. That's why folks like us never 'ave a chance, cause we start with nothin', and twice nothin' 's still nothin'. Idn't it? Mind you, not that some of it is not our fault."
medium		eye-level		Eddie: "Cheer you up Hilda, the good fight is not over yet."
close-up	zoom	eye-level		Hilda: "I sometimes think it never started for me, Eddie. Do you know, in order of preference I've always wanted a diamond ring, a set of pure silk underwear, a cheque book and a new oven ... What reminds me, what do you want for your dinner?"
medium				
pan to the right				Eddie: "Oh I, eh, I'll get a snack in the Rovers."
close-up	zoom			Hilda: "Oh, right."
full		eye-level	noise of the vacuum cleaner	

Visual Segments								
Sequence				Subsequence (Scene)		Shot		
Nr	Dur	Setting	Personae	Nr	Plot	Nr	Dur	Objects
5		continued		1	Ken. Deirdre says she cannot do that at the moment and entreats him to be patient.	1		Deirdre switches off the vacuum cleaner - comes to the phone - takes up the receiver and puts it to her ear - she talks and turns round while still talking.
						2	27 sec	Deirdre with the receiver at her ear - still talking
				2	On hearing Ken and Tracey coming Deirdre quickly finishes her telephone conversation to receive her husband and daughter at the door. When they have entered the living-room Deirdre asks Ken whether he found anything out from Alf why he was not accepted for the job. Ken very unenthusiastically answers in the negative, which upsets Deirdre.	1	16 sec	Deirdre puts the receiver down and goes a few steps to the front door to receive Ken and Tracey. She takes Tracey's coat- Ken turns to hang up his coat on a hanger. Then they go, one after the other through the door into the living-room - Deirdre is last, she hesitates a few seconds.
						2	14 sec	The three are now in the living-room - Tracey is sitting already at the left side of the round table. Ken also takes a chair and sits down. Deirdre first stands behind Ken - then she goes past him. After he has sat down she places herself on his left side so that she is standing between Ken and Tracey. Ken while (leafing through the newspaper) and Deirdre talk.

			Acoustic and Linguistic Segments
Shot		sound effect	Dialogeu
Type/camera movem./cam. angle			
	eye-level	the tele-phone rings	
zoom			
medium			Deirdre: "Hello..." Voice from the phone: "It's Mike!" Deirdre: "Oh, hello Mike!" Mike: "Is it allright to talk?" Deirdre: "Hm, well not really, Ken and Tracey will be back any minute." Mike: "Well what's happening about what we decided?" Deirdre: "Well, nothing really..." Mike: "Why not?"
close-up	eye-level		Deirde: "It's difficult Mike. I can't just tell Ken I'm leavin'. I am not just like that. Not with things like they are at the moment." Mike: "You promised you would." Deirdre: "Well, I just can't Mike." Mike: "Ha ... Well, what about this weekend?" Deirdre: "Well, ' doesn't look as if it's gonna to be easy to get away for the weekend either." Mike: "'re you sure you wanted to?" Deirdre: "'course I wanted to. Wha ... you just have to be patient with me, Mike. You just 'ave to give me more time." Mike: "Well, it's not easy." Deirdre: "It's not easy for me either. Look I'll 'ave to go they 're 'ere."
close-up	pan to right	eye-level	the door clicks	Deirdre: " 'ey!"
	zoom			
medium			Ken: "Hey!" Deirdre: "'had a good day at school, love?" Tracey: "Yeah!" Deirdre: "What did you draw? Anythin'?" Tracey: " A dinosaur."
medium (large)			Deirdre: "Oh, did ya! Bu' I bet you can't draw horses as well as I can, haha." Tracey: "I bet I can!"
	pan to left			
medium (large)	eye-level		
medium	eye-level	normal back-ground noise	
slight pan to left			
zoom (in)			Deirdre: "'as Alf managed to find out anything about the job?"
			Ken: "No!" Deirdre: "Can't he?"
			Ken: "Well, he's trying. I'm not sure if I want him to find out why not. I mean, it is not gonna to make any difference now, is it. It's academic ..."

	Visual Segments

Sequence				Subsequence (Scene)		Shot		
Nr	Dur	Setting	Personae	Nr	Plot	Nr	Dur	Objects
5		continued			continued	3	4 sec	Deirdre (silent and upset)
6	1 m 57 sec	The Rover's Return The Rover's Return is a conventional English pub. It displays a mixture of old-fashioned and glossy modern things. The tap-room consists of a large bar with side-pieces, and an area with tables and chairs. Behind the bar there are a door leading to the publican's living-quarters and shelves with glasses and bottles. Near the taps on the bar there are small flashy screens with the names of the different kind of beers in illuminated letters. Opposite the bar there is an opaque glass door leading straight on to the street. The tap-room is decorated with an ochre wallpaper with rhombic pattern; the pattern of the curtains matches the pattern of the wallpaper.	Eddie Yeats, Marion, Suzie Birchal, Bet Lynch, Mike Baldwin, Len Fairclough, Fred Gee	1	Eddie and Marion are standing at the bar of the Rover's Return being served by Suzie. Eddie teases Suzie who replies in a snooty manner. Marion retaliates on his behalf before she follows Eddie to a seat in a corner.	1	6 sec	Eddie Yeats and Marion at the bar. Suzie (profile) serving from behind the bar.
						2	6 sec	Suzie
						3	3 sec	Marion and Eddie
						4	1 sec	Suzie
						5	13 sec	Marion and Eddie (smiling). They go over to the table behind them. While Mike and Len enter through outside door.
				2	Behind the bar Suzie has words with Bet Lynch and stifles Fred Gee's attempt to chat her up. While serving Len Fairclough and Mike Baldwin Bet talks about the nature of men and the remoteness of the street.	1	32 sec	Suzie and Bet Lynch behind the bar - when Bet sees Mike and Len, she goes to that part of the bar where Mike and Len place themselves - Suzie looks upset - Fred comes from customers' area and talks to her - Suzie answers and leaves him
						2	7 sec	Bet behind the bar (frontal) - Len (seen from behind) and Mike (from the side) in front of bar.
						3	2 sec	Len and Mike (seen from front) (in the background someone opens the outside door)
						4	4 sec	The same as in 2

Shot		sound effect	Dialogue
			Acoustic and Linguistic Segments
Type/camera movem./cam. angle			
close-up	eye-level		Deirdre sighs
medium	eye-level	normal back-ground noise in a pub	Eddie: "Wasn't I right? Ain't I a tonic in the morning? Doesn't my coming round put a big smile on your day?"
close-up	eye-level		Suzie: "No! Do ya know why I thin' you come round every mornin'? To get your eye full."
medium (small)	eye-level		Marion: "He can only see what somebody lets him see, can't he."
close-up	eye-level		Suzie: "Hm ..."
medium (small)	eye-level		Eddie: "You 'll get a bit quick, when you 're housed with that all day, wouldn't you."
medium		normal b. g. n.	Marion: "I'm not a woman for nought, you know." Eddie: "You can say that again! Hey, come over there. I've somethin' to show ya." Marion: "Surprise?" Eddie: "Yes, sort of."
medium (small) pan to right eye-level			Bet: "It's allright love, I'll serve them. I know wha' they want."
pan to left			Suzie: "Has she got her own customers, or what?"
			Fred: "Oh, take no notice of that Lynch, love. Makes ya sick, eh. It's a big fault of hers, a'ways sniffin' round the fellers. Now I was thinkin' Suze ..." Suzie: (snooty) "What?" Fred: "When we finish, and it's all nice quiet, I wondered if you'd like a little spin in the country in the Rover, you know. A little ... little cream cheese somewhere. Possibly tea and crumpies ..." Suzie: "Oh, I'm sorry Fred. I'm slimmin'." Fred: "Oh."
medium	eye-level		Bet (to Len and Mike): "I'm right, aren't I. Men really do prefer the svelte mature woman to a young bit of fluff, don't they?"
medium (small)			Len: "No!"
medium	eye-level		Bet: "And I hope your vest runs off without you, Fair-clough! (to Mike) S'ppose you agree with it?"

			Visual Segments					

		Sequence			Subsequence (Scene)		Shot	
Nr	Dur	Setting	Personae	Nr	Plot	Nr	Dur	Objects
6		On the wall opposite the door near the bar there is a dartboard.		2	continued	5	2 sec	Mike with a glass of Scotch
						6	2 sec	The same as in 2
						7	1 sec	Mike - shaking his head
						8	5 sec	Bet behind the bar - Len (seen from behind) and Mike (seen from the side) in front of the bar (the same as in 2, 4 + 6)
						9	2 sec	Len
						10	8 sec	Mike and Len (seen from behind) in front of the bar - Bet (frontal) behind the bar
						11	4 sec	Len and Mike (seen frontal) in front of the bar
						12	4 sec	the same as in 10 only Mike is not in the frame anymore
						13	15 sec	Len and Mike laughing (somebody opens the door in the background)
7	1 m 22 sec	At the corner where Coronation Street crosses another street. It is wet outside and the sky is bleak. The street-corner belongs to two rather quiet side-streets	Stan Ogden and the manager of the local bank	1	Stan Ogden approaches the manager of the local bank in the street to ask for another loan when the bank has just closed for lunch. The bank mangager's answer is reserved and chilly.	1	21 sec	The window of the bank - the bank manager comes out of the building - closes door and steps onto the pavement where Stan is waiting for him (in the background a woman is seen walking by). The two talk

		Acoustic and Linguistic Segments	
Shot	sound effect		Dialogue
Type/camera movem./cam. angle			
close-up eye-level			Mike: "Hm?"
medium (small) eye-level			Bet: (brusque) "Forget it. What's new?" Len: "Not much."
close-up eye-level			Mike: "Nothin'."
medium (small) eye-level			Bet: "There must be somethin'. I mean the world just doesn't come to a stop, just because it's February. When 're you goin' skiin'?"
medium (small) eye-level			Len: "Skiin'?"
medium (small) eye-level			Bet: "Wha', somebody 's skiin', aren't they? I mean they 're on the tellie every Sunday. They 're on front of all the holiday brochures all white teeth and tans, lookin' like great admirals."
medium eye-level			Len: "I don't know anybody who'd go skiin'!" Mike: "Nor me."
medium (small) eye-level			Bet: "God, I sometimes think this place is cut off from the rest off th' world, it has no connection!"
medium eye-level			Len: "What's the matter with her? Now, what's the matter with you?" Mike: "Usual thing, mate." Len: "Aah! When you're married you're save from things like that." Mike: "Do you reckon?" Len: "Hm!"
close-up zoom- out medium pan to left eye-level further pan to left	normal b. g. n. in a calm side-street during lunch-time		Stan: "Eh, there Mr. Colfax? Have you got a minute?" Bank Manager: "Just closed for lunch, Mr. Ogden, twelve thirty to one thirty. You got to have hours."
medium			Stan: "Yeah, well, it won't take a minute, you see. I was wondering, eh, if you 'd see the way clear. Well, I was wonderin', eh if by any chance, you, eh, could manage another few quid .... I 've got a medical bill due, you see?"

		Visual Segments						
		Sequence			Subsequence (Scene)		Shot	
Nr	Dur	Setting	Personae	Nr	Plot	Nr	Dur	Objects
7		but in the background a busier main road is visible. The area is completely built up.		1	continued	2	4 sec	bank manager
						3	3 sec	Stan
						4	6 sec	bank m. - looks down, then nodds
						5	3 sec	Stan
						6	4 sec	bank manager (sneers)
						7	3 sec	the two talking (somebody walking by)
						8	10 sec	bank m. turns round to point at the bank
						9	1 sec	Stan (silent)
						10	6 sec	bank manager
						11	4 sec	Stan
						12	6 sec	Stan and bank m. - b. m. walks off (to right hand side) Stan alone - makes a frustrated gesture
						13	9 sec	b. m. (seen from behind) walking down a wet and rainy street - title (end of part one)
C	2 m 35 sec	Commercials on Anglia TV			A Finger of Fudge (19 sec) Chum (Dog Food) (31 sec) Fix it (Do-It-Yourself Magazine) (30 sec) Access (Credit Card) (31 sec) Eggs (30 sec) Home City (Carpet and Furniture Sale) (14 sec)			

		Acoustic and Linguistic Segments	
Shot		sound effect	Dialogue
Type/camera movem./cam. angle			
close-up	eye-level		Bank Manager: (incredulously) "Medical bill?"
close-up	eye-level		Stan: "Yeah, well, It's my back. I'm havin' it done private-like you know."
close-up	eye-level		B.M.: "You 're not in BUPA (1) then?"
close-up	eye-level		Stan: "I did join the RAC (2)!"
close-up	eye-level		B.M.: "Mr. Ogden you know the position as well as I do, before I can let you have any more I 've got to see the colour of what I have let you have already.
medium	eye-level		
close-up	eye-level		This isn't OXFAM (3) you know. I 'm not a registered charity." [(1) British United Provident Association (the largest private Health Insurance Association)
close-up	eye-level		(2) Royal Automobil Club (3) Oxford Committee for Famine Relief]
close-up	eye-level		B.M.: "I 'm what you might call the local branch of the International Monetary Fund. And what 's wrong with that?"
close-up	eye-level		Stan: "Nothin'."
medium	eye-level	Signature Tune	B.M.: "Hm."
long	eye-level		

Visual Segments								
Sequence				Subsequence (Scene)		Shot		
Nr	Dur	Setting	Personae	Nr	Plot	Nr	Dur	Objects
8	58 sec	Alf Robert's corner shop	Deirdre, Alf and Mike	1	The lunch hour is over and Deirdre has returned to Alf's shop where Mike Baldwin turns up briefly. Alf again mentions Ken's lost job opportunity and then mentions the incident between Mike and Ken in the shop earlier in the day.	1	6 sec	title (part two) the door of Alf's shop (from the inside) - a man leaves the shop (he is only seen from behind) Deirdre enters the shop almost at the same time
						2	7 sec	Alf behind the counter (frontal) talks to Deirdre - Deirdre goes past him into the backroom / Alf continues talking
						3	5 sec	Mike opens the door
						4	1 sec	Alf and Deirdre behind the counter (Deirdre looks apprehensive)
						5	2 sec	Mike walks out again
						6	38 sec	Alf and Deirdre behind the counter (frontal) - they talk -
						7		Eventually Deirdre goes into the backroom - Alf goes on talking (turns his head so that she can hear him) - Deirdre returns to her place
9	11m 47 sec	The Rover's Return	Fred, Eddie, Stan, Len, Bet and Suzie plus anonymous customers	1	Stan appears in the pub and joins Eddie and Len at the bar. When he tries to buy a beer on credit Fred Gee reacts in a very aggressive manner. To stop an escalation of the row, Len pays for the beer before he and Eddie leave.	1	15 sec	Stan enters the pub through the front door - he passes other customers and joins Eddie and Len who are standing at the bar (seen in half profile) - Fred serves behind the bar (half profile)

		Acoustic and Linguistic Segments	
Shot		sound effect	Dialogue
Type/camera movem./cam. angle			
		Signature Tune door bell	
medium	eye-level	normal b. g. n.	
medium	eye-level		Alf: "Hello, you 're soon, aren't you?" Deirdre: "I don't think so." Alf: "Not that I 'm not glad to see you, though."
medium	eye-level		Mike: "Whatta' I doin'? I got some cigars this mornin'. I must be loosin' me grip. Sorry 'bout that. See you."
medium	eye-level		
medium	eye-level		Alf: "See, even the big tycoons can be absent-minded." Deirdre: (apprehensive) "Yeah." Alf: "Hey, listen, I hope Ken don't think I let him down."
medium	eye-level		Deirdre: "Hm?" Alf: "Well, not finding out why he didn't get the job." Deirdre: "Oh, no I 'm sure he doesn't." Alf: "Well, I will find out, you know. He 's very down, isn't he? I mean, he even had Mike there, giving him some symp'thy this morning." Deirdre: (surprised) "Mike was?" Alf: "Yeah, somethin' he said, I s'ppose. I mean he said, he 'd find a job somewhere else you know. He was trying to cheer him up, I expect. But he won't, will he?" Deirdre: "No." Alf: "Look I 'm goin' into town hall this afternoon. I'll try, and find out then .... Did you hear what I said?" Deirdre: "Yeah, thanks very much, Alf, that's great." Alf: "There 's nothin' wrong, is there?" Deirdre: "No, o'course not."
medium pan to left further pan to left zoom out	eye-level	normal b. g. n. in a pub	Eddie: "You 're a late scholar, aren't you Stanley?" Fred: "Oh, give over. He 'd been in the leash of a donkey, weren't you, Stanley?" Stan: "Give us a pint, please, and it 'll be the first for today!" Fred: "Oh, and the rest..."

Visual Segments								
Sequence				Subsequence (Scene)		Shot		
Nr	Dur	Setting	Personae	Nr	Plot	Nr	Dur	Objects
9		continued		1	continued	2	10 sec	Stan is talking to Eddie
						3	12 sec	Len, Eddie, Stan and Fred (he brings Stan's beer, takes it away again but when Len pays for it he lets Stan have it).
						4	4 sec	Fred (profile) talking to Stan
						5	4 sec	Stan (arguing with Fred)
						6	2 sec	Fred (very angry and aggressive)
						7	2 sec	all four are seen (half from the side) Len interferes to pacify the two
						8	6 sec	Fred - he is still angry - turns round and goes to the opposite side of the bar
						9	11 sec	Stan, Len and Eddie talking - eventually Len leaves - Stan, Eddie alone - then Eddie leaves , as well.

Shot		sound effect	Dialogue
			Acoustic and Linguistic Segments
Type/camera movem./cam. angle			
medium (small)	eye-level	n. b. g. n.	Stan: (whispering) "Hey, lend us a quid, will ya. I only had about two sandwiches this morning, I 'm skinned." Eddie: "Oh, flippin' 'eck, Stanley, I can't keep subsidizing your hollow legs, you know, Stanley." Stan: "It's only a quid ..." Eddie: "No."
medium (large) zoom	eye-level		Fred: "Here you go, fifty-two ..." Stan: (obsequiously) "Can I have it on scrap?" Fred: (angry) "Oh, give over, will you ..." Len: "It's all right. I haven't paid you on this dinner, have I, Stanley."
medium			Stan: "Oh, thanks mate!"
close-up	eye-level		Fred: "By 'eck Oggy, you must have a long stockin' somewhere, the amount of money you spend for the amount of time you spend in here."
medium (small)	eye-level		Stan: (furiously) "You don't know Gee, do you. You sell your ale and keep your gob shut!"
medium (small)	eye-level		Fred: "I'll shut your gob in a minute, if you talk to me like that!!"
medium	eye-level		Len: "Allright, that 's enough now!"
medium (small)	eye-level		Fred: "Allright, allright, I might be standin' behind this bar, but I 'm not everybody's flippin'rubbin'rag."
medium slight pan to right zoom-in	eye-level		Eddie: "You nearly had your good looks spoiled there, Stanley." Stan: "Well, he couldn't do it, could he!" Eddie: "Oh, we are upset, aren't we." Len: "I 'm goin', I can't stand the sight of blood."
medium (small)			Eddie: "Me, too."

Visual Segments								
Sequence				Subsequence (Scene)		Shot		
Nr	Dur	Setting	Personae	Nr	Plot	Nr	Dur	Objects
9		continued		2	Behind the bar Bet starts a row with Suzie who has had Fred on her side, about Suzie's going to the Chemist during working hours.	1	6 sec	Fred is leaning on the bar - Bet joins him - the two talk
						2	1 sec	Stan is shown leaning sadly over the bar
						3	2 sec	Bet and Fred as in 1
						4	3 sec	Stan like in 2 - in the background Suzie is seen opening the front-door and walking in
						5	27 sec	Bet and Fred as before - Suzie arrives where they are - she talks to them, then starts arguing with Bet -
								Fred goes to a different side of the bar
								Suzie and Bet alone / rowing - Suzie eventually goes to the backroom behind the bar - Bet alone for a moment / she shouts in Fred's direction
						6	2 sec	Stan still leaning over the bar - behind him, Fred's hands are seen placing empty glasses on the counter

Shot		sound effect	Dialogue
			Acoustic and Linguistic Segments
Type/camera movem./cam. angle			
medium	eye-level	normal b. g. n.	Bet: "Did I 'ear voices raised just now?" Fred: "It's that Oggy, idn't it. Just got mad for no reason."
medium	eye-level		Bet: "He looks more like pathetic to me." Fred: "Yeah."
medium	eye-level		
medium			
medium	eye-level		Bet: (sarcasticly) "You know I knew there was a body missing but I couldn't quite bring it to mind ... Where the 'eck do 'ya think you 've been." Suzie: (innocently) "I only went out to the chemist." Bet: (sarcasticly) "Went out to Folly Filler (1), did we?"
slight pan to left			Suzie: (snooty) "That's what the chemist had t'do as well. He said you bought the last hundred weight! Anyway, Fred said I could nip out, didn't you Fred?" Fred: "Yeah well, it was quiet."
zoom-in			Bet: "You'd say it was allright for her to mug a fairy." Fred: "Bah.." [(1) a chain of chemist shops]
medium	eye-level		Suzie: (in a derisive manner) "Is it my fault that I'm young and beautiful?" Bet: (emphatic) "You'll have to book your ideas up, lady, when Mrs. Walker gets back."
zoom-in			
medium (small)			Bet: (to Fred) "And you can shut up at all!!"
medium	eye-level		

Visual Segments							
Sequence				Subsequence (Scene)		Shot	
Nr	Dur	Setting	Personae	Nr	Plot	Nr	Dur	Objects

Nr	Dur	Setting	Personae	Nr	Plot	Nr	Dur	Objects
10	1 m 48 sec	At the Ogden's	Stan, Hilda	1	Hilda is just about to leave for another cleaning job and is again complaining to Eddie about her hard lot and their lack of money when Stan comes in to be immediately rebuked by Hilda.	1	54 sec	Eddie is sitting in the foreground of the frame / reading a tabloid paper - in the background Hilda can be seen hurrying to get ready to go out - she approaches Eddie holding out her empty purse - Stan enters through the lobby - Hilda starts nagging
								- Hilda leaves
								- Stan puts his jacket on the table - addresses Eddie
				2	After Hilda has left, Eddie hands over ten pounds to Stan to give to Hilda when she comes back. But Stan immediately starts to make his way to the pub, which is prevented by Eddie.	2	1 sec	Eddie turns towards Stan and answers
						3	53 sec	Stan goes towards the kitchen door and enters the kitchen but reappears after a few seconds and takes a chair at the table - Eddie is still sitting in his armchair with the paper - he talks to Stan - eventually Eddie gets up, walks over to Stan, takes out a ten-pound note and gives it to Stan - Eddie now takes a seat at the right side of the table - the two talk - Eddie gives Stan a sharp look - Stan gets up to go to the kitchen again

		Acoustic and Linguistic Segments
Shot	**sound effect**	**Dialogue**
Type/camera movem./cam. angle		
medium　　　　　　eye-level	normal b. g. n.	Hilda: "No sooner I finish one job, I'm off for another. Th' story of my life is that. You read about people like me in books about the old days. But my mother never put in the hours I do, nor her mother before her. And what are the Unions after, ha? 35 hour week, I do a 35 hour day. What 'ave I got to show for it?"
zoom-in pan to right		Hilda: "Look! Just look in that purse. Wha' do ya see?" Eddie: "Not a lot." Hilda: "No, a few copper and we're s'pposed to live till Friday off that, three of us."
zoom-out pan to left further pan to left		Hilda: "Oh well, 'ere 'e is, the scarlet pimpernel. We seek 'im 'ere, we seek 'im there, one place we don't 've never to seek 'im 's where there 's any chance for 'im to do a job of work. Don't s'ppose you 've any brass for me?" Stan: (obsequiously) "No." Hilda: "No, what am I goin' to do with you Stanley. I'm beginning to think you beyond redemption, I'm honest."
		Stan: "'d ya 'ave any dinner?" Eddie: "'had some in th' Rovers." Stan: "Ah."
medium　　　　　　eye-level (small)		
medium　zoom-out　eye-level (large)　pan to left		
zoom-in		Eddie: "You 're not eatin' then?" Stan: "That tin of sardines 's open in there, I don't fancy 'em."
pan to right		
pan to left		Eddie: "'ere 's a tenner.'
camera moves down zoom-in medium (small)		Stan: "What 's tha' for?" Eddie: "For most of it's for Hilda. Give it to her when she comes home, tell her you 've collected a few bob off the round! Allright?" Stan: "Oh, thanks, mate." Eddie: "Right, so now you can go in the kitchen and make yourself a sardine sandy, and you can make one for me anow!" Stan: "'course now, I'll be goin' to Rovers." (Eddie looks daggers at him) Stan: (in an obedient manner) "No."

								Visual Segments		
		Sequence			**Subsequence (Scene)**			**Shot**		
Nr	Dur	Setting	Personae	Nr	Plot		Nr	Dur	Objects	
11	2 m 1 sec	In the corner-shop	Deirdre and Emily	1	Deirdre serves Emily in the shop who again tries to give her the advice to discontinue the relationship with Mike. Emily leaves the shop when Alf returns from his Council meeting.		1	6 sec	Deirdre behind the counter / she is serving Emily who stands in front of the counter (both are depicted in profile) - Deirdre eventually goes to one of the shelves on her left to get a loaf of bread which she hands to Emily	
							2	4 sec	Emily (seen from behind) and Deirdre (frontal)	
							3	3 sec	Emily	
				2	Alf tells Deirdre that he found out the reason for Ken's not getting the job. According to his information, it was mainly due to his apparent lack of energy and enthusiasm.		1	2 sec	Deirdre and Emily as in 2	
							2	10 sec	Emily	
							3	3 sec	Deirdre	
							4	4 sec	Emily looking down to her bag	
							5	7 sec	Deirdre	
							6	6 sec	Emily - she turns her head because Alf comes in through outside door - Alf walks past Emily	
							7	5 sec	Alf arrives where Deirdre is behind the counter (he gives her a meaningful glance) - he goes past her into the backroom, Deirdre (looks worried)	
							8	24 sec	Emily and Deirdre talking	
									Emily turns round to leave the shop	

		Acoustic and Linguistic Segments	
Shot		sound effect	Dialogue
Type/camera movem./cam. angle			
medium (large)	eye-level	normal b. g. n.	Emily: "Could I have my loaf, please."
pan to left			Deirdre: "Yeah .... Here you go, love, 27 1/2 p., please."
medium	eye-level		Emily: "I understand, you know Deirdre."
			Deirdre: "Do you?"
close-up	eye-level		Emily: "Strange as it may seem to you, I do. Life is a vale of tears, you know and trashing about can make it a lot worse."
medium	eye-level		
close-up	eye-level		
close-up	eye-level		Deirde: "Well, you mean ...eh, just grin and bear it?"
close-up	eye-level		Emily: "Something like that. And just cherish the good times."
close-up	eye-level		Deirdre: "Well, Mike thinks the opposite. He thinks you should grap what you can and he thinks that's more me, too."
medium	eye-level	door bell	Emily: "He would, wouldn't he."
			Alf: "Emily!" Emily: "Hello!"
medium (small)	eye-level		
medium (small)	eye-level	door bell	Emily: "I didn't mean that the way it sounded. But well, Mike is a free agent, isn't he. And you are not, Deirdre. That's the truth. Unpalatable though it may be. The last thing you want, my sort of advice, isn't it? Bye...."

			Visual Segments						

Sequence			**Subsequence (Scene)**			**Shot**			

Nr	Dur	Setting	Personae	Nr	Plot	Nr	Dur	Objects
11		continued		2	continued	1	48 sec	Deirdre is alone in the shop / she still stands behind the counter - the door behind her opens / Alf enters - Alf and Deirdre talk
								Deirdre is in tears
								- she goes into the back-room - Alf sighs
12	1 m 50 sec	Elsie Tanner's house	Elsie, Suzie and Marion	1	When Elsie comes home she finds Marion preparing the evening meal, though it would have been Suzie's turn. But Suzie arrives late with a new pair of shoes. In the course of the ensuing row Elsie reminds Suzie that she is two weeks in array with her rent and threatens to throw her out if she does not do her share of housework. But Suzie reacts as if unimpressed and in her usual callousness.	1	7 sec	Elsie enters the kitchen living-room from the lobby - she walks towards the kitchen part
						2	14 sec	She arrives at the sink where Marion is doing the washing-up - the two talk
						3	5 sec	Marion
						4	10 sec	Elsie and Marion
						5	5 sec	Suzie comes in the same way as Elsie did

		Acoustic and Linguistic Segments	
Shot		sound effect	Dialogue
Type/camera movem./cam. angle			

Shot			sound effect	Dialogue
medium	eye-level			
medium (small)	zoom-in			Alf: "Have you been busy?" Deirdre: "No, not specially." Alf: "Deirdre ....!" Deirdre: "Yeah, you found somethin' out, haven't you, about the job." Alf: "Yes, I have." Deirdre: "Well, go on, why didn't he get it?" Alf: "He 's not going to like it." Deirdre: "Why?" Alf: "He had actually got the qualifications for the job. But they, that is the committee that do the appointments, they seemed to think he got no ... gumption, I s'ppose you could call it. Get up and go, you know, drive, energy. They thought his attitude was all wrong. I mean they want a man of actions who'd make things num. And for all he's very clever but Ken don't do that, does he, make things num. Shall I tell him? I will if you like. But I needn't say anything, if you think it kinder."
	pan to right zoom-in			Deirdre: "I'll see, thanks Alf."
medium	pan to right	eye-level	normal b. g. n.	
medium	zoom	eye-level		Elsie: "What's going on?" Marion: "I'm makin' the tea, aren't I. Am I allright?" Elsie: "Yes, sure you are. But why isn't Fanny Fly by now doing it?" Marion: (in an angry voice) "She is not in!" Elsie: "Oh God, she doesn't change, does she. She was just like that when she was 'ere before. Young Gail was a mug."
medium (small)	eye-level		Suzie is heard coming	Marion: "You mean like I am now." Elsie: "Yeah." Marion: "Oh, come on Elsie. How much longer do ya think she is goin' to stop 'ere?" Elsie: "Don't ask me. It could be six months or she could do a bug tonight if she felt like it."
medium	eye-level			Marion: "Hm, don't raise me 'opes." Elsie: "Hang on a minute, she comes now. If you don't like bad language put your fingers in your ears."
medium	pan to right	eye-level		Suzie: "Hello! Something smells good."

Visual Segments								
Sequence				Subsequence (Scene)				
Nr	Dur	Setting	Personae	Nr	Plot	Nr	Dur	Objects
12		continued		1	continued	6	49 sec	Suzie arrives in the kitchen part - the three women remain there and argue
								Suzie takes out her new shoes -
								Elsie wags her finger at Suzie
								Marion is standing at the oven / she turns round to face Suzie -
								all three are rowing -
								Suzie and Elsie
								Marion and Elsie
								all three again
						7	2 sec	Suzie
						8	1 sec	Elsie and Marion
						9	3 sec	Suzie (profile) and Elsie's wagging finger

		Acoustic and Linguistic Segments
Shot	**sound effect**	**Dialogue**
Type/camera movem./cam. angle		
medium eye-level		Elsie: "Where do you think you've been?" Suzie: "Shopping! I bought the most beautiful pair of shoes. Red!" Elsie: (in a very angry voice) "Why weren't you 'ere getting us teas?" Suzie (innocently) "Was it my turn?" Elsie: "Oh, you know damned well, it was your turn."
		Suzie: "Oh, I'm sorry. I thought it was tomorrow, honestly. 'ey, aren't they lovely. Look!" Elsie: "Now, look madam, if you don't do your share of cookin' and all that, then you 're on your bike, and I mean it!"
		Suzie: "Oh, Elsie, I will do my share, really, I will. I mean, I like it here. I like you, I like Marion, just can't stand her binman, that's it." Elsie: "Oh!" Marion: "Just do leave Eddie out of this! Allright is Eddie!" Suzie: (snooty) "Then keep 'im out of th' house!" Marion: "He 's got as much right here as you have!" Suzie: "The only reason he comes here is to clock me in
pan to left		my nighty!"
		Marion: "He 's not like that, Eddie!"
zoom-in		Suzie: "He is normal, isn't he? Or isn't he?" Marion: "'course he is normal!" Suzie: "Oh and how would you know!" Marion: "Now, listen ..."
pan to right zoom-in pan to left		Elsie: "Now, shut up the pair of you. I' ve had a hard day's work and want a bit of peace and quiet ...! (Suzie and Marion are still shouting)
zoom-out		
medium eye-level (small)		Suzie: "Oh, get on with the tea, will you! Do you know how many pairs of shoes I have got now? Four!"
medium eye-level (small)		Elsie: "I tell you what I haven't got, madam. From you I haven't got next week's rent or last week's!"
medium eye-level (small)		Suzie: "Wow, first thing's first, Elsie! You spent enough on shoes in your time, didn't you, haha."

							Visual Segments	

		Sequence				**Subsequence (Scene)**		**Shot**	
Nr	Dur	Setting	Personae	Nr	Plot		Nr	Dur	Objects
12		continued		1	continued		10	3 sec	Elsie and Marion alone
13	4 m 1 sec	At Ken and Deirdre Barlow's house	Ken and Deirdre	1	When Deirdre returns home from work she finds Ken still in a very depressed mood. Deirdre reproaches Ken with not being enthusiastic enough. Still hesitant she tells Ken the reason which Alf found out why he did not get the job. In the course of the ensuing heated discussion Deirdre eventually also confronts Ken with her relationship to Mike. Ken is shocked.		1	4 sec	Ken is watching television in the dark (frontal)
							2	16 sec	Ken watching television (now seen in profile) - Deirdre comes in from the lobby - switches on the light - walks into the middle of the room - takes her coat off - she talks to Ken (with arms akimbo)
							3	34 sec	Deirdre turns round and goes into the kitchen - Ken's face is visible when Deirdre passes him - then only his face is visible - he turns his head and talks into the direction of the kitchen
							4	14 sec	Deirdre returns from the kitchen - for a moment she remains standing in the kitchen door and listens to Ken, then she starts talking and goes closer to where Ken is sitting
							5	18 sec	Ken is sitting in the foreground
									Deirdre is standing diagonally to him, with a packet of frozen food in one of her hands, which she bangs on the table (full of anger) - the two argue with each other

		Acoustic and Linguistic Segments
Shot	**sound effect**	**Dialogue**
Type/camera movem./cam. angle		
medium (small) eye-level		Marion: (full of anger) "I bunk her one before I'm much older!" Elsie: (also very angry) "You have to get in a queue first, love, you have to get in a queue!"
medium (small) eye-level	sound of television	
medium (large) (Deirdre's eye-level)		Deirdre: "What do ya sit in the dark?" Ken: "Watching tellie ..." Deirdre: "This early?" Ken: "Started with the news." Deirdre: "Tracey havin' tea around at Net's. What do you want?" Ken: "Whatever is going."
Deirdre's eye-level		Deirdre: "I think there is some chops, okay?" Ken: "Yeah, fine, fine .....(pause)."
medium pan to left zoom-in		
medium (small) Ken's eye-level		Ken: "...I don't suppose there is any news from Alf?"
		Deirdre: (from the kitchen) "Eh ... no." Ken: "Not that it matters, not that it matters a jot. It's not going to change anything .... This is my life, a crummy job in a crummy town. God knows how I came by it. This wasn't the idea, not the idea at all. The idea was success, achievement, satisfaction, a rounded life. But somewhere on the way I strayed from the road and I won't get back on it now."
medium (small) eye-level		Deirdre: "Can ya 'ear yaself, can ya?"
		Ken: "What?"
		Deirdre: "You 're pathetic! There 's nothin' wrong with your life that a little - I don't know - enthusiasm wouldn't put right!"
medium Deirdre's eye-level	sound of the TV	Ken: "I was enthusiastic about the job but they turned me down."
		Deirdre: "Allright! So be enthusiastic about the next one you apply for!" Ken: "But what 's the point? I was right for that job, perfect. But I wasn't lucky. I 've never been lucky. Just look at my record, one disaster after the other!

Visual Segments							
Sequence				Subsequence (Scene)		Shot	
Nr	Dur	Setting	Personae	Nr	Plot	Nr	Dur	Objects
13		continued		1	continued	6	16 sec	Ken
						7	3 sec	Deirdre (angry)
						8	1 sec	Ken
						9	1 sec	Deirdre
						10	3 sec	Ken
						11	5 sec	Deirdre
						12	9 sec	Ken - first silent - then he switches the TV off and looks to Deirdre
						13	7 sec	Deirdre
						14	1 sec	Ken
						15	9 sec	Deirdre
						16	1 sec	Ken
						17	2 sec	Deirdre
						18	8 sec	Ken (shouting)
						19	2 sec	Deirdre (silent and fearful)
						20	18 sec	Ken
						21	18 sec	Ken (profile) sitting - Deirdre standing diagonally to him (as in 5)
						22	3 sec	Ken
						23	2 sec	Deirdre (shouting with great anger) - her face is distorted

		Acoustic and Linguistic Segments	
Shot		**sound effect**	**Dialogue**
Type/camera movem./cam. angle			
close-up	eye-level		Okay, so that's the way it is. What's the point in trying? Why not just face facts and let the waves role over me till the last syllable of recorded time."
close-up	eye-level		Deirdre: "Not getting that job had nothin' to do with luck."
close-up	eye-level		Ken: "How would you know?"
close-up	eye-level		Deirdre: "I just know."
close-up	eye-level		Ken: "How?"
close-up	eye-level	normal b. g. n.	Deirdre: "Alf (pause) ... has found out somethin'."
close-up zoom-out	eye-level		
medium (small)			Ken: "And? Well, come on, why didn't I get it?"
close-up	eye-level		Deirdre: "You (pause) just didn't 'ave enough go about you."
close-up	eye-level		Ken: "Enough go ..."
close-up	eye-level		Deirdre: ".... Enough life, enough enthusiasm. That's just the impression you gave apparently. Oh, very clever, very intellectual, but ..."
close-up	eye-level		Ken: "Boring!"
close-up	eye-level	normal b. g. n.	Deirdre: "It 's as good a word as any."
close-up	eye-level		Ken: (in a loud voice) "Oh, yes it is! It is the in-word, isn't it. Anything that isn't witty, swinging or trendy, is boring!"
close-up	eye-level		Ken: (shouting) "I'm boring! And there 's just nothing I can do about it. Because the great tragedy is that I'm not aware of it. I
close-up	eye-level		happen to think that I'm a great guy. (pause) But apparently I'm wrong. Well, so be it."
medium	Deirdre's eye-level		Deirdre: "And that's it?" Ken: "That's it." Deirdre: "What about me? What about my life? I don't wanna boring life, I don't wanna just go through the
close-up	eye-level		motions!" Ken: "There 's nothing wrong with your life. Your life is rounded, you got a family, a home, a job and friends.
close-up	eye-level		I mean what's wrong with that?" Deirdre: "It 's not enough, Ken!"

Visual Segments								
Sequence				Subsequence (Scene)		Shot		
Nr	Dur	Setting	Personae	Nr		Nr	Dur	Objects
13		continued		1	continued	24	2 sec	Ken
						25	7 sec	Deirdre (her face turns pale)
						26	3 sec	Ken
						27	4 sec	Deirdre
						28	7 sec	Ken (stunned, almost hateful)
						29	3 sec	Deirdre
						30	8 sec	Ken
						31	4 sec	Deirdre
						32	6 sec	Ken (silent)
14	59 sec	Closing Sequence: Outside in the open air				1		roofs and chimneys of a long row of houses with credit titles

Shot	sound effect	Dialogue
Type/camera movem./cam. angle		
close-up eye-level		Ken: "But what else do you want, hmm?"
close-up eye-level		Deirdre: "What I found ..."
close-up eye-level		Ken: "What's that?"
close-up eye-level		Deirdre: "Somebody else."
close-up eye-level		Ken: "Who?"
close-up eye-level		Deirdre: "Mike ... Mike Baldwin."
close-up eye-level		Ken: "But that was before ..."
close-up eye-level		Deirdre: "It's now ..."
close-up eye-level		
long bird-eye view	Signature Tune	